Brain Fitness
at Work

Brain Fitness
at Work

Unlock your mind's potential and achieve peak performance

Judith Jewell

Part of the **MYRiAD** series

First published in Great Britain in 2005 by
Hamlyn, a division of Octopus Publishing Group Ltd

This edition published in 2009 by Bounty Books,
a division of Octopus Publishing Group Ltd
Endeavour House,
189 Shaftesbury Avenue,
London WC2H 8JY
www.octopusbooks.co.uk

Reprinted 2011

An Hachette UK Company
www.hachette.co.uk

This material was originally published as
Brain Fitness @ Work in 2003

ISBN: 978-0-753719-01-5

A CIP catalogue record for this book is available from the British Library

Printed and bound in China

CONTENTS

Introduction 6

Warm-up exercises 8

1 HOW OUR BRAINS WORK 10

2 TYPES OF THINKING 24

3 PACKING YOUR MENTAL BRIEFCASE 34

4 GETTING DOWN TO WORK 44

5 POWER UP YOUR THINKING 52

6 MAXIMIZE YOUR MEMORY 68

7 DEALING WITH STRESS 86

8 CREATIVITY AT WORK 96

9 COMMUNICATING YOUR IDEAS 108

CONCLUSION 118

Answers 138

Index 142

Acknowledgments 144

Introduction

Why do some people always seem to be full of clever ideas? Why are some people able to 'think on their feet'? And why are other people always the first to remember exactly what was said at last month's meeting?

Were they simply born smarter, quicker and more alert than the rest of us? Or could it be that they have realized that brains are like every other part of our bodies – and can be exercised and stretched and improved?

Like most people, I spent many years without thinking about how my brain worked. I just got on with school, college and then work, assuming that sometimes I would come up with ideas – and sometimes I wouldn't. I knew I was quite creative – people told me my drawing was good and I got good marks for some of my poems – and I scored well in maths and science, most of the time. But I do not recall ever being taught how to get the best out of my brain, or how to sharpen up my multiple intelligences or how to maximize my memory.

Science is providing more answers, and generating even more questions about the way our minds and memories work. We are now becoming more aware that creativity isn't confined to traditional areas. In addition, people are less willing to be judged solely on academic achievement.

Our brains have vast potential – we need a way to unlock it

This book is the result of many years' experience of using my brain at work as a management consultant, and 20 years of education before that. It is the product of all that I have read and learned and found out. It reflects stories and experiences from my own life and those of others who have shared their experiences with me. Where I have drawn directly on others' work, I have aimed to acknowledge it. But the sources of some of the ideas that my mind has provided me with are unacknowledged because I simply do not recall how I came by them. All I can do is thank the anonymous donors and hope that I have done those ideas justice.

This book is for *you* if ...

You have ever wondered why ... **you sometimes forget important things**

... **your best ideas come after the meeting**

... **you see things so differently from your colleagues**

You would like to improve ... **your resistance to distractions**

... **your ability to solve problems**

... **the way your meetings run**

You want to find out ... **all the different ways in which you are intelligent**

... **how you can heighten your five senses**

... **how to make sure you always communicate clearly**

You enjoy ... **looking at things in new ways**

... **questionnaires that tell you about yourself**

... **stretching your mind**

Warm-up exercises

Try these exercises to get your brain limbered up. (The answers are on page 138):

◀1 How many squares are there in this picture?

2 What comes next in this sequence?

3 4 6 8 12 14

3 The answers to these clues are words that sound alike but are spelled differently, for example, FRUIT and TWO – PEAR and PAIR.

GOLF ACCESSORY	**PROHIBITED**
DRINK	**GROUP OF MUSICIANS**
NUMBER	**MAN**
ALSO	**POST**
COMPLETE	**CONCEITED**
PERFORATION	**BLOOD VESSEL**
PART OF A PLAY	**ROUGHLY STITCHED**
NOTICED	**DIPLOMACY**

◀4 What is the lowest number of coins you need to move to get the triangle pointing downwards?

5 Fill in the missing number ▶

6 Which two letters belong in the gap?

CN		LF	PV
DP		??	QX
ER		NJ	RZ

7 Each of three friends – Mr Carpenter, Mr Mason and Mr Painter – is engaged in a different occupation. By a strange coincidence, one is a carpenter, one is a mason and one a painter; but their names do not necessarily match their trades.

Assuming that only one of the following statements is true, who does what?

Mr Carpenter is not a painter

Mr Mason is not a carpenter

Mr Carpenter is a carpenter

Mr Mason is not a painter

8 What room does the head of Human Resources work in?

CHIEF EXECUTIVE	Room 28
MARKETING DIRECTOR	Room 29
FINANCE DIRECTOR	Room 27
HEAD OF HR	Room ?

9 Continue the sequence by adding H, I and J in the correct places:

A		E F	
	B C D		G

10 Martha has to get her two babies, Roger and Sara, as well as the family cat, out to the car. Because Martha has a broken arm, she can only carry either one baby or the cat at a time. Unfortunately, neither baby can be left alone with the cat because Sara pulls the cat's tail, causing general chaos, and the cat will shed white fur on Roger's new navy sailor suit. How does she manage to get everyone out to the car in as few round trips as possible?

1 HOW OUR BRAINS WORK

'People travel to wonder at the highest of mountains, at the huge waves of the sea, at the long course of rivers, at the vast compass of the ocean, at the circular motion of the stars and they pass by themselves without wondering.'

Saint Augustine of Hippo

The last great frontier – this is how many scientists describe their work on the brain and the mind. Research findings about how our brains work often make the news and yet the experts often seem to disagree about what the results of the research mean.

One thing everyone does agree on though is that our brains are incredibly powerful.

They may only be the size and weight of an oven-ready chicken but they enable us to:

- read the newspaper

- hear and understand what the person next to us is saying

- feel excited about our next holiday

- notice the smell of a bacon sandwich and that nagging pain in our right shoulder

What's more – we can probably do them all at the same time. This is because our brains can make more connections and patterns of thought than there are atoms in the universe.

How our brains are constructed

Our brains have evolved over many thousands of years into the complex organs that we now take for granted, and their development can be traced in how the different parts of them function today.

All of the original brain functions are controlled by what is known as our 'primitive' brain. This region is about the size of an apricot and governs our basic functions, such as blood circulation and digestion. It is also responsible for the 'fight or flight' response to danger, which determines whether we will stand up to a threat or run away. Scientists believe that when we are under stress, the other parts of our brain partially shut down and leave everything up to the primitive brain, which is why we can find it hard to think rationally when we feel 'up against it'.

The second part of our brain to develop was our 'mammalian brain' – the part that is also found in most mammals. Physically it sits around the primitive brain and takes charge of processing our emotions and long-term memories. It also processes the information collected through our senses and passes it up the line for decisions to be made.

Covering these two regions is our most advanced brain, the 'cerebral cortex', which makes up about 80 per cent of our brain area. This is the wrinkled covering that we most usually see in a jar in horror movies. It is responsible for complex movement patterns, language, thought, reasoning and things like appreciation of poetry and music.

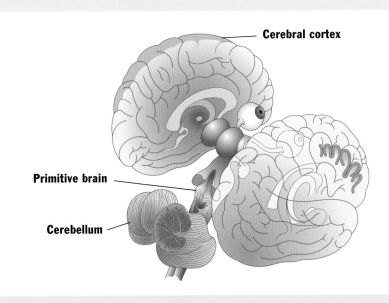

Cerebral cortex

Primitive brain

Cerebellum

Under the microscope

We all have millions of brain cells, called neurons, and each one is unique with its own special function. They use electrical impulses and chemical reactions to send and receive messages to and from the central nervous system and within the brain itself.

A neuron looks like a fantasy creature from outer space or a piece of plankton. Its central body has feathery arms, called dendrites, which receive and transmit the chemical information from and to other neurons, and translate it into electrical impulses. One longer dendrite – the axon – works like a lightning conductor. It collects all the impulses and sends them, at a speed of up to 120 metres (130 yards) per second, to relevant groups of neurons so that the appropriate reaction can take place.

Neurons store information and work together to generate actions and reactions. They work in groups, each controlling specific tasks. Each neuron has the potential for one million billion connections with other neurons – scientists estimate that on average we only use five per cent of our brain capacity in our lifetime.

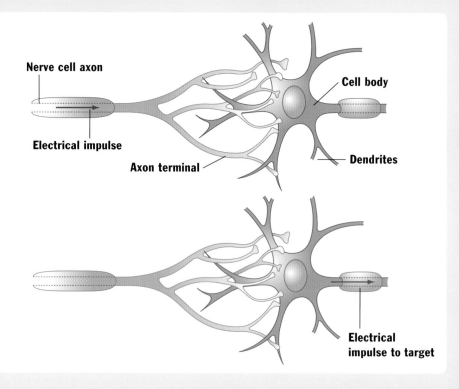

Nerve cell axon

Cell body

Electrical impulse

Axon terminal

Dendrites

Electrical impulse to target

The left and right hemispheres

For many years, people thought that we have two brains, just as we usually have two lungs or two kidneys. As long ago as ancient Egypt, people had noticed that the left side of the brain appeared to control the right side of the body and vice versa. Much more recently, in the 1960s, Roger Sperry (a psychobiologist at the California Institute of Technology) discovered that the two halves of the brain are associated with and control different activities.

The left side of our brain handles logical issues, and mathematical and sequential processing. It deals with details, organizes data and controls speech and writing.

The right side operates in a much more random and less organized way. It is the part of our brain that handles creativity, interpretation and metaphor and so on, and also works with our feelings, emotions and our intuition.

At one time, scientists believed that the various parts of the brain were entirely separate, but new thinking suggests that they can operate in a much more flexible way and that we can train different parts of our brains to learn new functions.

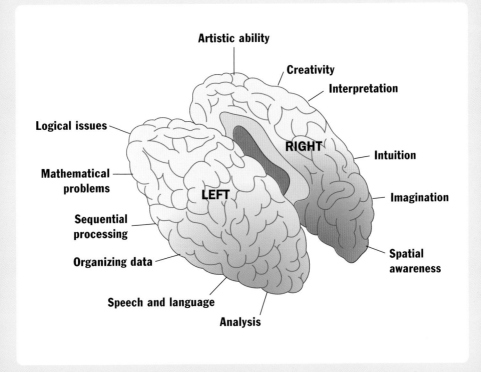

Artistic ability
Creativity
Interpretation
Logical issues
RIGHT
Intuition
Mathematical problems
LEFT
Imagination
Sequential processing
Organizing data
Spatial awareness
Speech and language
Analysis

Making sense of our senses

All day, every day, the world around us bombards us with information. Our five senses – sight, hearing, touch, smell and taste – pick up the messages that the objects and people around us are sending out, and our brains process them. And that is where the difficulty lies. How reliable are our senses?

The philosopher, René Descartes, noticed that we can be fooled by our senses. He conducted a simple experiment, which is easy to duplicate. Fill three bowls with water of different temperatures – one ice cold, one lukewarm and one as hot as you can stand. Put one hand each into the hot and cold bowls for one minute, then put both in the lukewarm water. Your brain is receiving different messages about the temperature of this tepid water from each hand: one tells you that the water is hot, the other that it is cool. Which is correct?

This unusual figure shows the parts of the body as they appear to the brain. The physical size of each part is related to the size of the area of the brain controlling that part's activity.

Even though you know, logically, that the water in the third bowl is at just one, uniform temperature, what the messages from your hands are telling you contradicts this. They are giving messages about the temperature relative to what they have been used to. It's usually enough to know that something is hot compared to normal, for example, so that our body can react accordingly, but our brains have the ability to take this further. It's one thing for the brain to be able to recognize that a cup of coffee is hot, but then experience and assumptions come into play to interpret that information, enabling you to make a decision about whether it's so hot that you'll scald yourself if you drink it.

How the brain controls the body

When you make any movement, the action starts as a burst of electrical nerve activity in the cerebral cortex. The motor cortex then sends out nerve signals destined for a certain part of the body. Parts that have very fine control, such as the fingers and lips, have bigger patches of motor cortex. The signals emerge from the base of the brain and flash down the spinal cord, along motor nerves to the muscles. Nerves that carry messages from brain to muscles are motor nerves.

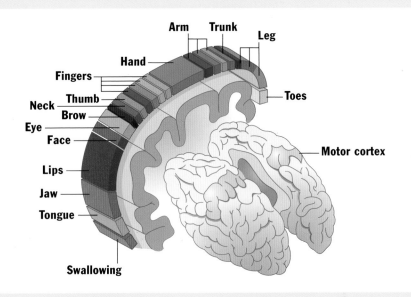

Personal perceptions

Even assuming that all your five senses are working well, what your brain tells you about the world will be different from what someone else would notice.

There are myriad opportunities for us to be fooled by our senses and to disagree with co-workers about what's going on. Just think about the last meeting you went to. Perhaps two people got into a discussion about what they thought they heard a senior manager say. Two other people couldn't agree on whether the room was too hot and perhaps you thought that the perfume the person next to you was wearing was rather cloying (they think it's alluring). And as for the taste of the new brand of coffee that the person running the meeting had chosen ...

Understanding and heightening your senses

There is good evidence that the more you are able to use your senses, the better your memory and thinking abilities will be. The activities below are designed to make you more aware of your senses, so that you can understand what they are telling you more readily.

SIGHT

We can distinguish millions of colours, distance, perspective, size and shape, using our 130 million photoreceptors. The visual cortex, which takes up 30 per cent of the cortex, is at the back of the head. Different groups of cells are responsible for distinguishing details such as colour and angles. This is why people with localized brain damage may lose only some aspects of their ability to process images. They may still be able to see the colour of a cup, but not to distinguish how near it is.

Activity

Look at something out of the window. What colours do you see? What shapes are any shadows making? Imagine turning the object through 90 degrees. What is on its front now? Close each eye in turn. How does this affect the size, shape and colour of your object?

HEARING

The structure of our hearing system is a marvel of miniaturization. Packed into about $2cm^3$ are a hydraulic balance system, a sound-wave analyser, a noise-reduction unit, a multi-channel transducer and a relay unit. When we speak, muscles in our middle ear contract to dampen our voices and incoming low-level frequencies. Otherwise, we wouldn't be able to talk and listen at the same time.

Activity

Spend two minutes listening. Notice all the sounds close to you. Then gradually bring in sounds from a wider radius. Try to listen to them above the nearer sounds. Finally, listen to the sounds in your own body and stop noticing sounds around you.

SMELL

In some ways, smell is a very simple sense. There are only 5 million receptors and most people can detect only 10,000 odours. Every time we breathe in, we bring microscopic bits of the outside world into contact with nerves in our noses. These nerves have one end dangling in the outside world and the other communicating with the brain. Smell's first stop is the brain's emotion-processing area. This is why smells are so good at evoking powerful memories and feelings.

Activity

Next time you are shopping, walk around a food market or the fresh food area of your usual supermarket. Identify three different smells, and notice what thoughts and feelings arise in connection with each.

TOUCH

Our skin measures about 2 square metres (21 square feet) and is the largest organ in our body. It has 200,000 receptors for cold, 500,000 for touch and 2,800,000 for pain, all unevenly distributed. The most sensitive parts of the skin can distinguish between separate points (like pencil tips) applied only 3mm (⅛in) apart. Like smell, touch is linked to our emotions.

Activity

Let yourself become aware of everything you are touching, either directly or indirectly – the texture of this book in your hand, the feel of your collar on your neck and your chair seat pressing up onto your thighs.

TASTE

This sense is in some ways our simplest; we certainly have fewer taste receptors (taste-buds) than any other type. They are renewed every ten days or so. We used to think there were only four tastes (sweet, sour, salty and bitter) but Japanese research has come up with 'umami' (related to glutamates) as a fifth. Taste is a survival tool – poisons are usually bitter, and unripe fruit is sour.

Activity

Next time you have a chance, try a food you haven't eaten before. Try to classify its taste by putting a little on the relevant parts of your tongue in turn: front – sweet, front sides – salty, back – bitter, far sides – sour.

So how clever are you?

Many people have grown up with the self-belief that they are either intelligent or they're not. From an early age we will have overheard things like: 'Your Suzie's very bright, isn't she? I'll bet she's got a high IQ,' or, 'Little Jimmy's smart – he'll go far with that IQ.' Alternatively, of course, we may have been unfortunate enough to hear less favourable remarks.

BUT WHAT IS 'IQ'?

The whole idea of certain types of intelligence being a measure of someone's worth or potential became popular around the start of the 20th century. William Stern and Alfred Binet designed tests to measure people's 'Intelligence Quotient' (IQ). These were based on language and numeracy. Some, now thankfully discredited, researchers suggested that people with higher scores must be superior to those with lower scores.

Collins English Dictionary defines intelligence as 'the capacity for understanding'. This concept of intelligence as simply being skilled at mental arithmetic is woefully limited. It is much more helpful to describe an 'intelligent' person as someone who can use their mind in a combination of ways.

MULTIPLE INTELLIGENCES

In the last 20 years or so, psychologists have been suggesting that we have more than one 'intelligence'. Howard Gardner is one of the most notable. Bill Lucas, of the Campaign for Learning, has helped to refine the idea of intelligences further and Daniel Goleman made the concept of Emotional Intelligence famous. Danah Zohar added Spiritual Intelligence to the debate.

The table opposite shows common characteristics of each type of intelligence and activities for improving each one.

THE 10 INTELLIGENCES

INTELLIGENCE	CHARACTERISTICS	ACTIVITIES TO ENHANCE THIS INTELLIGENCE
1 LINGUISTIC	A wide vocabulary and a good idea of correct spelling and grammar.	Choose a long word or a short phrase and see how many other words you can make with the letters.
2 MATHEMATICAL	Good at number puzzles and abstract problems. Understands statistics and notices when they're misleading.	Look for occurrences of numbers in everyday life – keep a running total on your way to work: 'Number 14 bus, plus the 9.05 train (919), plus 13th-floor lift button (932)'.
3 VISUAL	Good at diagrams and illustrations and aware of shape, colour and texture.	Imagine describing your job or a hobby to someone else without using words – what diagrams, maps, pictures would you use?
4 PHYSICAL	Enjoys physical activity. Is good with his or her hands and may use hand gestures when speaking.	At least once a day, move away from your work area and do something physical; for example, stretch up to the highest shelf in your office.
5 MUSICAL	Good at recognizing different rhythms and types of music and able to remember melodies.	Next time you listen to some music, either on purpose or by accident, try to pick out the different instruments.
6 SOCIAL	Enjoys being with other people, in both formal and informal settings. Good at noticing other people's moods and listening to others.	Find opportunities to talk and listen to someone you haven't communicated with before. Volunteer for an activity that involves talking to everyone, such as organizing a leaving card collection.
7 ENVIRONMENTAL	Good understanding of the natural world and interested in the environment.	Next time you walk somewhere, make a point of looking at the shapes of clouds, any greenery, animals and birds.
8 PRACTICAL	Good at sorting things out and putting things together. Interested in how theories work in practice.	Next time you need a small practical task doing, note down what stages you think you'd need to go through to do it yourself.
9 EMOTIONAL	Aware of their own feelings and moods, and how experiences affect them. May set personal goals and keep a diary or journal.	Once a week, spend time on your own and think about a recent event, such as a meeting. Then write how you felt at each stage.
10 SPIRITUAL	Aware of the values and principles that lie behind actions and concerned with fundamental questions about life.	Look for interviews in the media in which people talk about their values and beliefs. Notice their reasons for their views, and look for words that express them.

THE GENDER GAP?

It is obvious that there are many physical differences between men and women. The problem comes when someone suggests that such differences make one gender superior to the other.

We now know that while the male human brain weighs on average about ten per cent more than the female brain, certain areas in women's brains contain more nerve cells than men's. And we also know that, for as long as intelligence tests have been in use, women and men have consistently scored equally well.

Brain size doesn't really help us, therefore, to understand male and female thinking. It's probable that male and female brains work at the same capacity, but process information differently.

Using brain imaging equipment, scientists have observed that men and women complete the same tasks in similar times, with similar results, but that different parts of the brain are used. Other research shows that there are tasks that members of one sex perform more successfully than those of the other. For example, women can often recall sections of a text better than men, whereas men will perform better in tests that ask them to rotate an image mentally to solve a problem, such as finding their way around a town centre.

Activity

Think of a woman and a man that you know in your work environment. Notice how each of them operates in certain situations, and then think about how you work in the same circumstances. You are not making judgments now about which method is best, simply observing any differences and similarities. Of course, this won't tell you how all men and women would think in similar situations, but it will help you become more aware of different thinking styles. For example:

	JANE	JOHN	ME
Making decision about who to ask onto committee	Listened a lot, then asked lots of questions, but made few notes.	Had his own idea of preferred choice, but asked us all to speak in turn with our views.	Listed criteria, then made up my mind very quickly.

OUR BRAINS AND AGEING

Most of us have probably grown up with the notion that the brain starts its dying process almost as soon as we're born. It is true that many areas of our brains do not regenerate naturally, but, as we have already seen, much of the brain's function relies on the millions of interconnections between brain cells, not on how many actual brain cells we've got. It also looks as though the fact that older people's brains weigh less is more to do with dehydration than brain capability.

Scientists are now questioning earlier research that 'proved' that older people were less intelligent than younger people. Most of the tests simply gave groups of people the same time-limited IQ test. Older people got lower scores, so testers drew a simple conclusion – young people are cleverer than old people. Once testing became more sophisticated and such factors as someone's familiarity with IQ tests and their understanding of the language used, were taken into account, older people did equally well.

Unfortunately, the myth about loss of brain power as we grow older persists, both in Western culture generally and in the workplace in particular. Of course, many degenerative illnesses do strike older people, so most of us will be able to think of someone who has become confused or less able to think clearly than they once did. But it isn't an inevitable consequence of ageing – you will be able to think of many people, either famous or who you know personally, who seem to be getting better with age.

Activity: 'Do something different today'

Write this phrase boldly in whatever way suits your diary. For example, use a mini sticky note in a paper diary, or a flag in your electronic organizer. Keep moving the flag through the diary so that doing something differently becomes a daily habit. It doesn't have to be anything that takes a lot of extra time. You could:

- Use a different route to the photocopier.
- Choose a different magazine to read on your journey to work.
- Try a different sandwich filling.

Then spend a few minutes thinking about what that new experience has taught you.

Limber up – mental dexterity exercises

The answers are on page 139.

A piece of cake

What is the lowest number of straight cuts you need to make to divide this cake into eight equal pieces?

All in the family

At a wedding there were six people called Chris and this is how they were related to each other. Chris is Chris's cousin, Chris is Chris's husband's sister and Chris is married to Chris.

What is the highest number of women that could be present?

Count on it

The numbers in each triangle have the same relationship. Fill in the missing number.

Lost letters

Fill each bracket with a letter that fits on the end of the word on the left and fits at the start of the word on the right.

HEART( )EATER
PLANE( )AUGHT
SUPER( )LIGHT
LARGE( )OTTER

Country code

In this code, each country has a value. What is the value of Turkey?

THAILAND 13
AMERICA 10
TURKEY ?
CHILE 8

Lucky 13

Find another way to make 13 using the letters below.

ELEVEN
+
TWO

Follow on

What are the next two numbers in the sequence:

2, 11, 6, 19, 10, 27, 14, 35, ?, ?

Odd one out

Can you find the odd one out?

1 UUSTGA

2 AAYJURN

3 CHARM

4 DUSYTEA

5 LUYJ

6 PREESTMEB

2 TYPES OF THINKING

Like nearly everything else in this book, thinking can be thought about in lots of ways. Down the centuries great thinkers have applied their minds to finding out what goes on when we think.

WAYS OF THINKING

Every day we apply our brains to questions and problems, and there are many possible approaches to finding solutions. In fact, we often use more than one way of thinking at the same time:

- turning an idea over in your mind
- examining all sides of an argument
- reflecting on something that's happened
- looking for connections
- breaking a process into parts
- imagining what might happen in the future
- remembering something from the past
- being aware of what is happening around you

... and no doubt you can think of other methods that we use in our daily thinking schedule.

A different approach may provide the answer

When we are trying to find ways to keep our brains fit to deal with all the things that we have to cope with in our working day, it probably helps to simplify things a bit. Basically, there are two types of thinking that we could apply to the items in the list above: analytical and creative.

ANALYTICAL AND CREATIVE THINKING

	ANALYTICAL	CREATIVE
Mostly uses	logic, facts, figures, data	imagination, intuition
Approach	narrows things down, time-limited	widens things out, not time-limited
Method	vertical (deep, narrow, probing), linear	lateral (all ideas OK even those not thought to be linked)
Uses	building a case, drawing conclusions from data	breaking a stalemate, changing perceptions, challenging assumptions
Most active brain hemisphere	left	right

Activity

Choose a decision that you will soon have to make. It can be big (shall I move house?, for example) or small (shall I have coffee or tea?). Now think about the decision in the two different ways:

ANALYTICALLY	CREATIVELY
What is the current situation? What do I want? What are my criteria? What information do I have? What information do I need? What are my choices? Which choices match my criteria? Who will be able to help me implement the choice?	Imagine a time in the future when the decision has been made. Draw a picture of yourself successfully doing/using the solution. What feels like the best solution?

We'll look in detail at analytical and creative techniques later on. For now, just notice how different each way of thinking felt and make a note of any insights you actually got about the decision you were considering. It may have been only an exercise, but most people report that having the chance to focus on an issue does tend to bring some new thoughts to the surface.

How we organize our thinking

Don't eat the tablecloth

We all have ways of organizing our knowledge and experience, although we may not be conscious of them. Our ability to recognize and make judgments about things and then put them away in mental boxes helps us to cope with the world. For example, if we have a box in our mind marked 'food', we know what to do with the items on our plate at dinner time and we don't attempt to eat the tablecloth. We don't have to test every item around us to see what is edible.

Of course, this very ability to identify and compartmentalize is one of the things that can block our best thinking. We may use very simplistic labelling (for example, tastes good/tastes bad).

PREVIOUS EXPERIENCES

An individual's ability to use his or her thinking processes will partly depend on previous learning experiences. Remember how hard it was as a child to make up your mind about which sweets to choose in the sweetshop, especially if you were told to 'Hurry up'. Then, when you'd made a choice, you were asked, 'What did you choose that for? You'll make a mess.' In such simple and often kindly meant ways, we've all been discouraged from using our thinking processes and become distrustful of our ability to do so. We worry about taking too long and making wrong choices.

Anyone can think creatively

Our workplaces don't always help. Traditionally, analytical thinking has been valued more highly than creative thinking and many people have got out of the habit of even trying to think creatively.

QUESTIONNAIRE

Try this questionnaire to see where your true abilities lie. Read each pair of statements and mark which you prefer – they are not exact opposites. Please choose one, even if it is only a very slight preference.

A I spend some of every day 'pottering about'
B I hate wasting time

A When I have a decision to make, the first thing I do is make a drink
B When I have a decision to make, the first thing I do is to gather all the information I'll need

A I enjoy daydreaming
B I dislike daydreaming

A I revel in being a bit different
B I like to fit in with the crowd

A People might describe me as talkative
B People might describe me as thoughtful

A I read around a subject to find out what others think before I commit myself
B I make my mind up before finding out others' opinions

A I like using unusual words
B I like using precise words

A I prefer puzzles that could have lots of answers
B I don't really like doing puzzles

A I'm sensitive to the working environment – I can't think properly if my surroundings are unpleasant
B Once I'm concentrating on the job in hand, I hardly notice my surroundings

A I would like to be thought of as imaginative
B I would like to be thought of as logical

A I like to bounce ideas off other people
B I like to work out my own strategies before other people contribute

A I believe intuition has a place in decision-making
B I do not believe intuition has a place in decision-making

A I feel stressed if I'm asked to come up with a structured approach to a problem
B I feel stressed if I'm not given clear guidelines within which to work

A I like to hear what famous people think about current issues
B I'm not interested in what famous people think about current issues

A 'Big picture' questions are best for starting discussions
B Probing questions are best for getting to facts

A I like to be allowed to voice my opinions, even if they may be unpopular
B If I know that my opinion might be unpopular, I'll keep it to myself

A I like abstract ideas
B I like practical ideas

A I was not always happy at school, especially when I felt that the rules were constricting
B I found school rules helpful – they provide structure

A I like taking things apart to see how they work
B I like putting things together so that they work

A I like group creativity sessions
B I like thinking things through on my own

A I believe mistakes can be useful if they lead to fresh ideas
B I believe mistakes can be useful if they lead to getting things right

SCORING

Now tot up your scores to see where your true abilities lie.

Mostly As   **STRENGTHS** You have high creativity and will probably be able to generate ideas easily and work with hunches. You are comfortable with the ambiguous and get frustrated if you feel constrained. You do not mind being thought of as a bit unorthodox.
AREAS TO WORK ON You need to make sure that you don't miss detail, particularly if you're on your own.

Equal numbers of As and Bs   **STRENGTHS** You have a pretty balanced approach to thinking. You are equally happy working in a group or on your own, and you will probably feel comfortable using a range of thinking techniques.
AREAS TO WORK ON You need to make sure that you don't let the fear of taking a risk hold back your creativity.

Mostly Bs   **STRENGTHS** You have well-developed analytical skills and can understand complex sets of data. You like issues to be well defined and you get frustrated with vagueness. You are good at being methodical.
AREAS TO WORK ON You need to ensure that you listen well to others' ideas – they may reach the same decisions as you by different routes.

There is no right or wrong way of thinking

This questionnaire is not designed to be judgmental. There is no 'best' way to be. The important thing is to identify where your thinking skills may be lacking and to look for opportunities to try out thinking methods that you are unfamiliar with. You may have surprised yourself with your answers and come out with more As than you would have expected – in most sectors, even if we might like to be a bit unorthodox, it feels safer to conform. Current research is demonstrating that organizations that encourage their staff to use their creativity are more likely to succeed.

Learning

The concept of **learning**, as opposed to **teaching**, has rightly become very popular in recent years. You may be familiar with the old saying: 'You can lead a horse to water, but you cannot make it drink.' This describes how many people first experienced being taught. They were put into a classroom, and someone talked to them, probably at some length, about a subject. Whether the student learned anything in this scenario was a matter of chance. Perhaps enough facts would sink in to get through an examination, especially if there was some threat or promise attached. But generally, such methods of teaching have been shown to be largely a waste of time.

In fact, of course, we always do learn something from each experience. In the situation just described, it may be: 'Well, I've learned not to go to that class again without a novel to read behind my textbook.'

LEARNING FROM EXPERIENCE

When we learned to walk as children, we didn't find it necessary to go on a course, watch an instructional video or look on the web. No one sat us down and explained physiology to us. We just kept on having a go, falling over, finding things to hold on to and having another go. And we still learn like that as adults, however sophisticated we think we are.

Much of the time, we do not even realize that we are learning. We don't tend to use the language of learning in our everyday lives, but instead say things like:

'I'd like to have a go at that'

'I wonder why that happened'

'Next time, I'll try it another way'

LEARNING STYLES

Peter Honey and Alan Mumford have researched learning in many organizations over many years. They identified what they called an 'experiential learning cycle', and discovered that there are four 'learning styles', which can be plotted onto the cycle as shown. Most people will have a preference for one or other of these learning styles, although this doesn't mean they don't use the others. The trick is to get better at the others in order to learn throughout all the experiences that we have.

Stage 1
Having an experience
Activist

Stage 2
Reviewing the experience
Reflector

Stage 3
Concluding from the experience
Theorist

Stage 4
Planning the next steps
Pragmatist

ACTIVIST STYLE

- enjoy new experiences and being 'thrown in at the deep end'
- like the excitement of a drama or crisis
- respond well to ideas outside policy constraints
- need to bounce ideas off other people
- won't appreciate being told to read the manual before plugging in their new PC

THEORIST STYLE

- work well with theories and concepts
- enjoy being stretched intellectually
- respond well in structured situations
- don't appreciate doing things that don't have an apparent purpose
- don't like things that seem to them shallow or 'gimmicky'

REFLECTOR STYLE

- are good at painstaking research
- like having the chance to sit back and think
- appreciate having time to think before acting
- don't like being pushed into doing something without time to prepare
- are worried by crises and time pressure

PRAGMATIST STYLE

- are good at seeing links between concepts and their everyday use
- work well on practical activities like action plans
- respond well to the chance to put things into practice immediately
- need guidelines and instructions before having a go
- don't appreciate learning that's not immediately useful

Activity

Think back over the last week. Identify something that you have done which you would like to think of again as a 'learning experience'. It doesn't have to be a major event, like learning a new software package. It could be something like talking to a colleague. Then take it round the learning cycle. Make notes about each stage. For example:

1 Having the experience

Last Tuesday I spent an hour with Sue, talking about improving the post recording system. We'd both brought examples of ways in which we'd seen it done in our previous companies. We'd previously agreed to take the best bits from each system. We started the meeting off OK, but ended up having a bit of an argument and not agreeing on a new system.

2 Reviewing the experience

I listened well at first to what Sue had to say about her system. I got a bit irritated with her when she kept straying off the point and reminiscing about her old company. I think I'd done a bit more research than she had. I felt rather pressurized because I had to get away to pick my daughter up from nursery.

3 Concluding from the experience

I think we got into the argument because I wasn't very clear about why I was irritated. I went into the meeting having decided that 'my' system was the best.

4 Planning the next steps

In a similar situation, I'd be much clearer about my time pressures and more assertive if the other person goes off the point. With Sue, I need to explain why I felt frustrated. I need to make sure that I have the opportunity to go through my system too.

Of course, no one has enough time to go through this process this methodically after every experience. But if you get into the habit of doing it once in a while, and certainly more often mentally, you'll soon be far more of an all-round learner.

Personality type and thinking

You may have done various personality tests during your life. Sometimes you see the result and think, 'Yes, that's me, all right. It's uncanny.' At other times your reaction may be much more sceptical. In fact, it may actually be an aspect of your personality that's affecting your response to the test.

One of the most important things to remember whenever we think about personality types is that there is no 'best'. However, understanding ourselves and others in terms of personality types can explain why we get all our best ideas when we're working with some people and simply get frustrated when trying to work with others.

Carl Jung was the first to investigate how our personalities affect how we deal with information. He discovered that people fall into different groups depending on how they prefer to handle information (**S**ensors or I**N**tuitors) and make decisions (**T**hinkers and **F**eelers). As a shorthand, these are referred to as S, N, T, F. The initial N was chosen for the iNtuitors to avoid confusion with another aspect of Jung's work – the difference between Extroverts and Introverts.

WHAT DOES IT ALL MEAN?

Sensing and iNtuiting are about how we prefer to take in and process information. Sensing people will be likely to use their senses, while iNtuiting individuals are more likely to use insights and connections. Neither is better than the other, and each can use the other's style. If you are an S working with an N, you can complement each other well.

Thinking and Feeling are about how we prefer to make decisions. Ts are not 'unfeeling' and Fs are perfectly able to think. This is simply about which you're likely to use first. Both are rational, it's just that Ts and Fs have different ideas about what 'rational' means. Once again, neither is better than the other.

Activity

Which responses most closely match what you'd be thinking in the given situations? Choose an S or an N, and a T or an F each time.

1 A colleague brings her answerphone to you in pieces, after trying to fix it.

S: 'I know how these work. Hand it over and I'll put it back together for you.'

or

N: 'Have you checked in the manual? Have you rung the manufacturer? Has it happened before?'

and

T: 'Here's my manual, you can borrow it. You could try fixing it, or you could find out which would be cheaper, repair or replacement.'

or

F: 'Oh, poor you. Do you think you've missed many calls while it's been out of action? You can borrow mine if you need to.'

2 Your boss suggests a change to one of your procedures.

S: 'I can see how that would work.'

or

N: 'It's a bit like the way we used to do it in my previous company.'

and

T: 'It will work if we get the right software.'

or

F: 'I hope she's taken everyone's views into account.'

3 Your colleague asks how many people you think will come to the Friday lunchtime seminar you're organizing.

S: 'I'll have to check with all the other sections to get their attendance lists.'

or

N: 'Oh, about 40.'

and

T: '37.'

or

F: 'It probably depends on what else is going on that day and how tired people are at the end of the week.'

4 A bit of an argument is developing at the weekly meeting.

S: thinks: 'Why can't they keep to the point?'

or

N: switches off and gets on with a 'things to do' list.

and

T: thinks: 'They're not being very businesslike.'

or

F: thinks: 'How can I calm things down?'

3 PACKING YOUR MENTAL BRIEFCASE

'Pen, organizer, mobile phone, meeting agenda, magazine, apple, ideas, insights, reflections ...'

Do you ever give any thought to what mental skills you'll need for the day ahead? Most of us are quite used to the idea of making sure we've read the documents for the first meeting of the day, but we probably won't have thought, 'Oh, I'd better make sure my logical thinking is ready.'

Is your mind ready for the demands of the day ahead?

In the past, when someone started a new job, they'd get a job description (if they were lucky) and were just told to get on with it. Maybe this is a bit of an over-simplification, but many people over 45 would say that sounds like their experience.

Today, you are much more likely to have guidelines about how you're expected to work as well as what you're expected to do. Often, these expectations are set out in the form of 'competences'. Competences are statements about the abilities you're expected to demonstrate right across your job.

Have a look at the list of competences opposite. It may appear daunting at first, but if you look at it in terms of a typical day, you'll see that you're probably already coming up to expectations.

COMPETENCES

Initiative	Act on own initiative. Understand when action is needed.
Creativity	Challenge preconceived ideas. Find innovative approaches to problems.
Resilience	Maintain performance under pressure. Respond flexibly to short- and long-term changes in priorities.
Expertise and specialist skills	Continuously develop knowledge and skills relevant to this job, and consider development to the next career move.
Analysis and judgment	Recognize importance of information in relation to current issues. Evaluate and reach decisions and workable solutions.
Service delivery	Meet needs of internal and external customers. Seek out and offer new approaches.
Dealing with people	Act in a way that shows respect for others. Awareness of impact of own behaviour on others. Provide direction and management to others as appropriate. Work co-operatively and supportively with colleagues.
Communication	Express ideas and convey information clearly and confidently.

COMPETENCE DIARY

Have a look at your work diary for tomorrow.
Think about which competence you'll be using as you do each activity.

TIME	ACTIVITY	COMPETENCE
08.30	Arrive	
08.35	Coffee at desk. Read papers for meeting	Expertise and specialist skills
08.45	Meeting with Mike to decide budget strategy	Dealing with others, expertise, creativity
11.30	Brief June about budget	Communication

What you bring with you to this job

When we first looked for work, we were encouraged to include details of our outside interests on our job applications to give prospective employers an idea of what sort of people we were. Now, it is much more useful to describe outside activities in terms that employers will recognize as being useful in the workplace.

COMPETENCE DIARY

Emphasizing skills used outside the office that employers will find useful is particularly important for women who are returning to work after some years spent bringing up a family. For example, getting two children to and from school and activities becomes 'Organize and operate transport schedules'. This is not 'spin' because she would use the example of the school run in the interview. First, write as comprehensive a list as you can of all the things you do in your life. Think of things under the headings of: Home, School, Hobbies, Jobs, Community, Spiritual and any more you can think of:

HOME
Organize family's diary

Plan and shop for meals

Cook

Resolve conflicts

PREVIOUS JOBS
Waitress in college bar

Checkout operator at supermarket

Book-keeper

SCHOOL
Form prefect

Ran chess club

Organized sixth form fashion show

Took part in debating competition

Played recorder

HOBBIES
Reading fiction and biographies

Swimming

Going out with friends

Pottery class

COMMUNITY
Take the minutes of Parent Teachers Association committee

On rota to help at Cub Scouts

Used to volunteer at Samaritans

SPIRITUAL
Sing in gospel choir

Then, try to identify what thinking skills and competences you use in each, and add them to your list on the previous page. Now imagine you are presenting your brain portfolio to a prospective employer.
How are you going to sell yourself?

Emotional
Conflict handling
Counselling

Musical
Singing
Play instrument

Mathematical Intelligence
Budgets
Book-keeping
Chess

Visual
Fashion sense
Home decorating

Linguistic Intelligence
Debating
Reading
Committee minutes

Case Study

Suresh had worked for some years for a medium-sized distribution company. He felt that he was good at his job, and enjoyed it most of the time. He was, however, beginning to wonder whether he would progress further. He'd always fancied the idea of being a salesman.

One Friday, the company newsletter arrived on Suresh's desk and seemed to fall open at the 'Company Opportunities' page. The sales team was looking for a Junior Sales Rep. Suresh closed the page, thinking they would never consider him.

That evening, he had to be at his son's school at 7pm to chair the working party set up to look at the feasibility of the school buying a mini-bus.

On Saturday morning, Suresh went to visit the Chairman of the Chamber of Commerce. Suresh's community

newspaper needed advertisers and he wanted to convince the Chairman that local businesses would get customers this way.

Suresh told his wife about the ad for the sales team but how his experience would be too limited. She ticked off on her fingers all the areas of his life that Suresh could use to convince the Sales Manager he'd be good on the team.

'Initiative – great idea to approach the Chamber of Commerce. Selling abilities – look how you convinced the local authority to put up half the funds for the mini-bus. Teamwork – all the committees you're on. Dealing with people – remember how you sorted out that row at work?'

So Suresh spent the rest of Sunday updating his CV, writing his portfolio and filling in the application form.

Next Friday, he got the job.

Personal competence audit

This questionnaire will help to highlight where you're already demonstrating the competences and where you might need to develop. It may give you some insights or it might confirm what you already knew – or guessed.

It contains 40 statements. Think about yourself as widely as you like, both at work and outside the workplace, and circle A, B, C or D alongside each number in the scoring table opposite.

Circle A if you think the statement is always or nearly always true of you; if you strongly agree; if you always or nearly always behave or feel the way indicated by the statement.

Circle B if you think the statement is generally true of you; if you fairly definitely agree; if you quite often behave or feel the way indicated by the statement.

Circle C if you think the statement is occasionally true of you; if you partly agree; if you occasionally behave or feel the way indicated by the statement.

Circle D if you think the statement is definitely not true of you; if you disagree; if you hardly ever or never behave or feel the way indicated by the statement.

1   I am prepared to tackle tasks that other people ignore.
2   I use creative ways of looking at problems.
3   I admit to my mistakes and take action to prevent or minimize any problems caused by them.
4   I regularly attend seminars about subjects to do with my work.
5   I can quickly get to grips with large volumes of information.
6   I make sure that things I say will get done do get done.
7   People would describe me as fair and reasonable.
8   When I give other people verbal information, they say I am clear and concise.
9   I know how and where to get the resources I need to do my job.
10 I am interested in new approaches to tasks and I welcome ideas from other people.
11 People would describe me as someone who can 'think on their feet'.
12 I could describe my company's business and how it works to a newcomer.

13 If I'm involved in a project, I am aware of the stage we're at and how well it's going.

14 My customers, both inside and outside the organization, know what I can and cannot do for them.

15 When I'm working in a team, I take part in developing that team's goals and plans.

16 I do not have difficulty getting other people to understand my point of view.

17 When necessary, I take the initiative without waiting for direction from those above me.

18 I offer a range of solutions when I can.

19 I have a reputation as someone who delivers on time.

20 I belong to the business and specialist associations relevant to my work and go to their meetings whenever I can.

21 When I have to make a presentation or write a report, I spend time researching and preparing.

22 I work with my customers to help to identify and resolve problems.

23 When I'm working with other people, I like to make sure we all know what to expect from each other.

24 I recognize and avoid jargon and clichés in my speaking and writing.

25 If a situation has reached a stalemate, I take action to move it on.

26 I think all ideas are worth looking at, whoever suggests them.

27 I work effectively in stressful situations.

28 I am well-informed about what's going on in the world that might be relevant to my job.

29 I can identify which organizational objectives relate to my work.

30 I try to look for reasons to do something rather than reasons not to.

31 I am aware of the impact on other people of my behaviour and actions.

32 I speak at meetings on behalf of my team or organization.

33 I look for opportunities to take on responsibilities in new areas.

34 I often introduce new ideas at work.

35 When I'm under pressure, I still keep long-term priorities in mind.

36 I give consistent advice.

37 I base decisions on practical experience.

38 I identify the benefits in a situation for others as well as myself, aiming for a win-win outcome.

39 I prefer to get disagreements out into the open rather than have an uncomfortable atmosphere.

40 Colleagues often ask me to comment on their letters, reports and so on before they send them.

SCORING TABLE

									17 A	18 A	19 A	20 A	21 A	22 A	23 A	24 A
									B	B	B	B	B	B	B	B
									C	C	C	C	C	C	C	C
									D	D	D	D	D	D	D	D

1 A	2 A	3 A	4 A	5 A	6 A	7 A	8 A		25 A	26 A	27 A	28 A	29 A	30 A	31 A	32 A
B	B	B	B	B	B	B	B		B	B	B	B	B	B	B	B
C	C	C	C	C	C	C	C		C	C	C	C	C	C	C	C
D	D	D	D	D	D	D	D		D	D	D	D	D	D	D	D

9 A	10 A	11 A	12 A	13 A	14 A	15 A	16 A		33 A	34 A	35 A	36 A	37 A	38 A	39 A	40 A
B	B	B	B	B	B	B	B		B	B	B	B	B	B	B	B
C	C	C	C	C	C	C	C		C	C	C	C	C	C	C	C
D	D	D	D	D	D	D	D		D	D	D	D	D	D	D	D

SCORING

To calculate your score, give yourself 4 points for every A, 3 points for every B, 2 points for every C and 1 point for every D. Then add up the total number of points in each column. The eight columns correspond to the eight competences on page 35.

INTERPRETING YOUR RESULT

The questionnaire is designed so that the highest scores indicate competences in which you are already strong. The maximum score for any competence is 20 and the lowest possible is 5. Lower scores show where you may need to do some development work.

Look over your scores. Are there any that stand out as definitely low? Or are they all about the same? If two or three are definitely lower, then it would be a good idea to make these your priority development areas. If they are all about the same, choose the two or three competences that seem most relevant to your current job.

Of course, this questionnaire is wholly subjective, and you need to bear in mind that you are probably your own worst critic.

It's important to remember that development includes continuing with the things you're already doing well. As we've seen, we learn from experience, therefore identifying our existing skills so that we can transfer them to our weaker areas is also a vital activity.

COMPETENCE REVIEW AND ACTION PLAN

List the three competences that you are going to work on.

Now write a list of how each competence applies in your job.

Then write three things that you are going to do to develop each one. This may not be an easy task. After all, it's probably because you don't always know what to do in a particular competence area that's led to a low score in the first place. So you could use the questions that you answered with C or D as prompts for ideas if you are stuck.

The competence ladder

Think about something you currently do almost without thinking, such as driving a car. Even if you don't drive, you may find it a helpful analogy.

Before you even wanted to learn to drive, you saw cars moving along the streets. You had no idea what was involved in driving. Then came the day of your first lesson. All of a sudden, there's a huge amount to take in, about the car, other drivers, the road, the pedestrians. Somehow, you make it from A to B, but you aren't really driving yet – you're all too aware of all there is still to learn.

Soon, though, you're ready to take your test. You can do it, but you're going to have to concentrate like mad. You think through every manoeuvre, making sure you do everything in the right order.

Once you've passed, you can go out on the road on your own, and before too long you're able to drive while listening to the radio, talking to your passengers or enjoying the scenery – hardly thinking about the driving at all.

You've climbed the 'competence ladder', and when you reach the top, you may see other ladders stretching away into the distance.

NEW SKILLS WALL

UNCONSCIOUS COMPETENCE
I'm doing it without thinkng

CONSCIOUS INCOMPETENCE
I know what a lot I've got to learn

CONSCIOUS COMPETENCE
I can do it, but need to think about it

UNCONSCIOUS INCOMPETENCE
I don't even know what there is to learn

Making the most of your journey to work

It may be that you need your journey time to recharge your physical batteries. A little nap on the train can be very refreshing. Your favourite music in the car or your personal stereo may help you to relax. But sometimes a journey is just dead time. This is a waste if you want to arrive at work with your brain ready to go.

Activities to warm up your thinking

1 Imagine that you have the task of compiling the test questions for a quiz programme, using your own job as the competitor's chosen topic.

2 Focus on an impending task. Fill in this box:

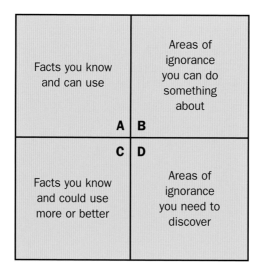

Facts you know and can use	Areas of ignorance you can do something about
A	**B**
C	**D**
Facts you know and could use more or better	Areas of ignorance you need to discover

How will you convert: Cs into As? Ds into Bs? Bs into As?

*Warm up your mental muscles
on the way to work and arrive
alert and prepared ...*

3 Think about what you did yesterday evening, even if it was simply watching TV. Take it round the **learning cycle** (see page 30–31). Identify at least one thing that you could say you've learned from it.

4 Imagine a situation that you're facing today. Put yourself into the picture.
What will you see as you look around?
What will you hear? Touch? Smell? Taste?

Now imagine one of the other people who'll be involved.
What will they see and hear as they look at you?

5 Choose a famous person from the current news, or that you can see pictured in someone's newspaper. Call to mind a problem that you are facing. How would that famous person solve it?

4 GETTING DOWN TO WORK

DISTRACTIONS

'I just get started and the phone rings.'
'Have you got a minute?'
'I know I had that file here somewhere.'

Recognize any of these? There are all sorts of distractions that can stop us working and thinking. Some of them are external – other people, and the environment in which we are working, distract us – and others are internal – we do them to ourselves. Even some of the external distractions are more about how we handle them than what other people do to us.

FIVE WAYS TO RECLAIM YOUR SPACE

1 Make sure your work space is a space – not just the top of a pile.
2 If you haven't read those torn-out newspaper articles in the three months since you saved them, you never will. Throw them away.
3 Aim for a full wastepaper basket and an empty desk every day.
4 Use a pad or notebook to record calls and messages – scraps of paper and sticky notes get buried.
5 Make sure your phone is on the side you don't write with – then you won't have to reach across and mess up your space every time you make a note while you're talking.

Whether you work at home or in an office, open plan or private space, behind a reception desk or a shop counter, you can have some control over your environment. Arrange your work space so that when you come to start some brain work you can get right to it.

FILING

The invention of the filing cabinet was a revolution in office life and meant we could now keep everything. And with the arrival of carbon paper and later the photocopier, we could keep duplicate copies of everything.

Research has shown that people ignore about 85 per cent of the paper they keep and that 45 per cent of it is also kept somewhere else by someone else. Put a note in your diary every week to spend 30 minutes going through the papers you have accumulated and work out which fall into the 'I'll never need this again' category or the 'Someone else has got this' category.

Work out a filing system that works for you – it doesn't have to be clever or elaborate. However, don't wait for the right time or the perfect system before you get organized – get on with it now.

Case Study

Jane decided to fulfil her dream and leave her organization to set up as a freelance personnel consultant. She brought home her box files and several carrier bags full of papers. She had a 'library' of magazine articles, presentation notes and folders, and was looking forward to having the time to develop a proper filing system.

She set aside a week to devise a perfect system, but every time she thought she'd cracked it she'd find a flaw. For instance, she put all her papers and articles about mission statements in one folder and those about in-house training schemes in another. Then she found a magazine article about how in-house training schemes help organizations fulfil their mission statements. She started a 'To think about later' pile. Soon this pile was bigger than all the rest.

Jane realized that while at work she'd managed with a simple set of box files with fairly general titles. Her real problem was that she hadn't filed papers and articles promptly. She decided to set aside half an hour a week to sort everything and file it into the most appropriate box. It didn't matter that the box called 'mission statements' might have some stuff that was only vaguely related – the point was that Jane no longer had teetering piles of papers all over her space.

Interruptions:
How to reduce them

The easiest way to reduce interruptions is not to have any.

This is not about refusing to speak to anyone who dares to ask you a question when you are working. It is about changing your mindset and reclassifying interruptions into:

Type A – part of my work
and
Type B – stopping me working

How many of the things you call 'interruptions' are actually a legitimate part of your job?

Case Study

Sue was Reception Manager in a busy, small hotel. As well as taking her turn on the reception desk, she supervised the other two receptionists and the three porters/maintenance staff. She organized the rotas, summarized all the time sheets and prepared monthly personnel returns.

On one particularly busy afternoon, Sue had just settled down to the monthly task of summarizing the time sheets when a man appeared at the reception desk. Angela, the duty receptionist, was temporarily away from the desk. With a big sigh, Sue approached the guest. 'I'll never get this finished if I keep getting interrupted,' she said, not quite under her breath.

Luckily, the man was a regular guest and was not offended. 'Sue,' he said 'I'm not an interruption to your work – I AM your work!'

For Sue, checking in guests was a 'Type A' interruption.

KEEP A TIME LOG FOR A WEEK

Yes, it takes time, but the pay-offs can be enormous. Be as precise (and honest) as possible. Do the timekeeping as you go through the day, but save the analysis until the end of the week.

1 Make a note of the time you start each activity.
2 Describe what you are doing in a few words.
3 Note the time each interruption starts, including times you interrupt yourself.
  (You will need to explain this politely to some of the other people who interrupt you.)
4 Note the time you resume the original activity.

For example, a section of your completed time log might look like this:
10.20 Got out papers for meeting.
10.25 Started reading financial summary report ready for discussion at meeting.
10.35 Fred came in with printout I needed for meeting. We clarified a couple of figures.
10.46 Picked up report again and started reading.
10.50 Went to water cooler for drink. Bumped into Bill and chatted about last night's game.
11.05 Picked up report again and started reading.
11.20 Packed up papers and left for meeting.

Without the time log you might have thought, 'I spent nearly an hour reading that financial summary report. No wonder I didn't get much else done this morning.' In fact, you actually spent about 29 minutes on it, because of two interruptions. The first was a 'Type A' (Fred – 11 minutes) and the second a 'Type B' (Bill – 15 minutes).
  By looking at a few typical days, you will be able to see how much of your time is taken up by the two types of interruption, and how much time you could save by cutting down on 'Type B' interruptions.

REDUCE THE NUMBER OF TYPE B INTERRUPTIONS

Drop-in visitors

How welcoming is the area immediately around your work space?
  Is there an empty chair right next to your desk? This chair is saying to anyone who comes in, 'Please sit on me.'

Do you face the direction from which people approach, so that you feel tempted to look up and smile? Your smile is saying, 'Please interrupt me – my work is less important than yours.'

If possible, rearrange your work space so that approaching people are not in your line of sight, and lose the spare chair or put it somewhere less convenient for visitors.

Of course, your job may be all about welcoming people into your space. If you are a staff welfare officer, you can hardly barricade yourself in. If you are the office cashier, the cash office has to be open. But you can advertise your 'opening hours' – just make sure you stick to them so that all your colleagues get the message.

Voicemails

Do people phone you rather than look things up for themselves? Are there dozens of messages when you return to your desk?

Put a long message on your voicemail. Research has shown that most callers don't wait for the end of a long message. (You may get more phone calls when you are answering your phone, but it should cut down the time you spend on voicemails.)

REDUCE THE LENGTH OF EACH TYPE B INTERRUPTION

Have a sand-filled egg timer by your phone. Turn it over at the start of each call. It will help you keep track of the length of your conversations. (If your phone has a call duration display, use that.)

Use your **assertiveness** skills. If someone asks, 'Have you got a minute?', reply, 'Yes, but only a minute – I really must finish this report,' or even, 'No, not at the moment. I must finish this report. I'll pop round to see you later.'

When someone comes into your space, move round to greet them – they will spend less time chatting if you have taken control and are not behind your desk. (It is also easier to end a phone call if you have moved away – so stand up or move your chair back.)

A final thought – how many of your colleagues' Type B interruptions are you responsible for?

Distractions:
We do to ourselves

Many people feel that they lose the ability to **concentrate** as they get older. It's not age that causes most of the changes in our abilities – it's our responses to other factors. At work, we may have become too busy for long periods of concentration, or perhaps we have lost interest or enthusiasm for the subject we need to focus on. The good news is that everyone has the ability to concentrate – we just need to harness that ability when we need it. Remember when you got completely absorbed in a book or a film, or deeply engrossed in a hobby or activity. OK, so writing the minutes of the last team meeting may not be quite as much fun as helping your daughter put together her model boat, but you can use your skills and achieve a similar sense of satisfaction.

Let's use the analogy of running.

ON YOUR MARKS

Different events need different training schedules. Is the task you're facing more like a sprint or a marathon? Is it more like a solo or a team event? What equipment will you need? It is easy to stop ourselves getting down to work when we haven't got ready properly.

If a piece of work is going to need you to be at the peak of your concentration, set aside time for it when you know you'll be at your best. Shut the door and put your answerphone on. Make sure that your chair is comfortable and that everything you need, such as a notepad, reference books or files with the relevant information, is in easy reach. Make sure that you have enough light and air.

Many people remember that they did their best concentrating in their student days with music playing in the background. If this would help you, use a personal stereo. This has the added advantage of blocking out unwanted external distractions.

GET SET

Now is the moment to focus on where you are going with this work:

What is the overall objective?

Are there any short- and medium-term goals?

What outcomes do you want?

Which standards will be applied?

Which skills and attributes are you going to use?

What new things will you learn along the way?

Activity

Ask yourself the questions above about a task you have to tackle, in this instance writing up the minutes of last Friday's team meeting.

What is the overall objective?

• To get the minutes written and circulated by the end of this week

Are there any short- or medium-term goals?

• To decide on a format that's not too formal but gets all the action points down

• To get a first draft ready by the end of this morning

• To get Raj, our team leader, to read through this by the end of today

What outcomes do you want?

• A move away from the overly formal style of minutes that none of us read

• For people to think I can do a good job on this

Which standards will be applied?

• It doesn't need to be perfect first time

• People will remember the way Joan used to do them, but that's OK

Which skills and attributes are you going to use?

• My meetings expertise from my last job

• The stuff I learned on the Plain English course last month

What new things will you learn along the way?

• Different ways in which different team leaders like things done

• How to summarize lots of discussion into short action points

Of course, you don't have to write all this down – but it may help you focus. It will also make the task seem more manageable and might even make a dull one more interesting.

GO!

Set yourself realistic targets

It would be crazy for most people to say to themselves, 'I'll work at this non-stop for three hours or until I've finished.' It is much better to work for bursts of half an hour, have short breaks and come back to it feeling refreshed.

Give yourself a little treat

Reward yourself when you have achieved each of your targets. These don't need to be in the form of food or too much caffeine or nicotine. Taking a five-minute breath of air or letting yourself read a couple of pages of your magazine would both be good ways of refreshing yourself and encouraging the creativity to flow again for the next lap.

Keep a distraction list

When something else pops into your mind, such as 'Must remember a card for Jeff', write it down on your distraction list to deal with later. Then you can forget about it and get on with your main task.

Vary your activities

It's not only young children who find concentrating and sitting still for long periods difficult. Try to include a variety of activities in your task – highlighting, reading, writing, walking around while thinking and so on.

Use your distraction productively

This is a useful technique when you are thinking. Notice when you have become distracted and use the distraction to make a connection with the thing that you are meant to be thinking about. For example, when you are summarizing a presentation you attended, you notice a woman walking along the street outside with a huge dog. Big dog – strength – strong arguments in favour of the subject ... and you are back on track. Don't struggle to find a connection – it doesn't matter if one doesn't come. The point is, you are soon back with your main task. In fact, this simple technique will soon become second nature and will not only help you to resist distractions, but will lead you to some good creative thinking.

Approach your work as a relay race, not a marathon

5 POWER UP YOUR THINKING

As we've seen, our brains work by making connections, and it is important to remove blocks. Just as electricity doesn't work if insulation tape is wrapped around the plug, your thought processes won't work if you have thinking blocks.

GET RID OF YOUR THINKING BLOCKS

Let's have a look at some of the most common forms of thinking block, in order to understand and then get rid of them.

Perceptual shut windows

How you look at something affects how well you'll be able to think about it. Is the glass half empty or half full? These are some of the ways in which failure to look at a problem with an open mind means that we can't work out what the underlying problem is:

- Stereotyping, and limiting the problem too closely. For example, 'We are short-staffed because younger workers haven't got the same loyalty as older people.'
- Failure to isolate the issues. For example, 'We're short of staff and customer complaints are rising.'
- Inability to see other viewpoints. For example, 'No one likes a shop with no music in the background.'
- 'That's not logical.' What if it worked anyway?

Emotional insulating tape

We need to be aware of our feelings in any situation, because they can be a guide as to how best to deal with what is happening. However, feelings can block our thinking if we let them take over.

- Fear of looking silly or sounding foolish. How often have you sat in a meeting, not quite clear what's going on, but been afraid to ask?

- Fear of taking a risk. You may have got strong messages in the past about not stepping out of line.
- Anger that your values are being challenged. For example, in a discussion that seems to be heading towards a decision to reduce staff numbers, you may feel so angry on behalf of the staff that you stop evaluating what is being said.
- Excitement about a possibility. Your judgment might be clouded by the chance to do something new.

Cultural barriers

We put these up when we have become overly sensitive about the prevailing culture so that we stop thinking 'the unthinkable'.

- Taboos. These arise when we think we can't entertain certain ideas. For example, in a new office with limited space, the only solution is to put Bill and Jane at the same workstation, but everyone knows they once had an affair, so we couldn't ...
- 'Thinking is a serious business.' We've heard: 'Quietly please, I'm thinking,' so often that anything that suggests that we might laugh or enjoy the process is too hard to take.
- 'We'd better follow the rules.' You won't be punished just for challenging the 'rules' in your mind.

Environmental blocks

We all know what conditions we need in order to do this. As we saw earlier, we can do a lot to take control of our environment.

Intellectual breakdowns

This is all about having the tools for the task.

- Inadequate thinking techniques. Most people never come across the correct techniques – unless they get a book.
- 'I'm not really qualified to contribute.' Perhaps you're not in terms of job skill or experience, but your idea might be the one needed.
- Lack of correct information. It is so frustrating to spend time sorting out a solution to an issue only to find out that one of our basic facts was wrong or incomplete. We need to make sure that information is based on fact and not assumptions or opinions.
- 'I'm just not creative.' This needs challenging every time it pops up. You may not have had much practice lately, that's all.

Problem or challenge

The first step in thinking about an issue is to check that you're thinking about the right thing, and if you're thinking with someone else, that you agree about what the issue actually is. As an example, here's a common problem:

'The trouble is, we need more space in this office.'

Actually, what we've just done is state a solution – more space. But what would we be using that space for? You may think we need more space to give us all more shelving options, but I'm expecting to squeeze in another desk.

REFRAMING

One great technique for finding solutions is called 'reframing'. This enables us:

1 To get a different perspective

It turns a problem into a challenge. All you need to do is turn the stated problem into a 'how to' statement. For example, 'We haven't got enough money to decorate the staff room,' becomes:

How to get the funding for the redecoration   or
How to reduce the cost of redecorating   or
How to get the materials for free   or
How to get someone else to pay for it   or
How to change our minds about needing it   or
How to find another way to improve   or
How to feel better about not doing it

2 To break a stalemate

It helps us to identify as much as possible that we agree on. For example, my company needs to be paid $50 a tonne to make a profit. Your company cannot afford to pay more than $48 a tonne.

What do we have in common? Cash limits and the need to stay in business. Let's think about:
Other ways we can save money.
Providing something to make up the shortfall.
Providing something to reduce costs.
Offering some of the product to another company.

3 To analyse a problem

It helps us to find out what the issues really are, making it possible to identify the positive aspects of the problem, and then see how they affect what we're trying to do. For example, if the problem appears to be: 'This room is very dark because of the tree outside the window', it helps to identify the **positive aspects** of this situation:
The tree is beautiful. So we're not talking about cutting it down.
The room is cool in the summer. So it's not even an air-conditioning problem.
It stops people staring in. So privacy's not the issue.
The room is gloomy. So perhaps the issue is how to brighten the room up.

THE MAGIC WAND TECHNIQUE

This is another type of reframing. Firstly, imagine that your fairy godmother has waved her magic wand and your problem has been solved. What can you now do that you couldn't do before? How does the world look now?

For example:
'I never have time to do any tidying up.'
Imagine the magic wand doing its stuff. You now have time to do the tidying. What is the issue now? **'I have time, but I don't know where I'm going to put everything.'**

Magic wand ...
'OK, I can see a system, but I've got too much stuff.' Ah, all along the issue has actually been that I keep so much stuff that tidying up becomes too daunting.

The stepping-stone guide to problem-solving

Stepping-stones across a river are usually fixed in place and order, but may not be in a straight line. So this is a helpful analogy for problem-solving.

When solving a problem, we use both the right and left brain hemispheres (see page 13). We need some **structure** and some **freedom** in order to arrive at the best solution. The following method is **logical** and **analytical** in itself, and uses **creative thinking** techniques along the way. It's quite a lengthy and detailed process, and won't be appropriate in full for every problem-solving situation you face, but do try to work through it completely now.

STEP 1 Clarify your problem

As we've seen, it's not always straightforward to work out exactly what the problem is. It is vital to make sure that the problem is something you want to tackle and that the solution is within your control – you wouldn't get very far with: 'My office isn't on a Caribbean island,' however systematic a method you used.
  Use the reframing techniques to get this step right for you.

STEP 2 Limit the scope of the problem

Are you tackling this for everyone in the company for the next five years or just the ten people in your office for the next six months?

STEP 3 Analyse the causes

Why is this a problem? Draw up a list of the most likely causes. Remember to avoid preconceived notions and stereotypes.

STEP 4 Generate possible solutions

Start 'brainstorming' by just noting down all the ideas you come up with. You're aiming to create as many ideas as possible. Resist the temptation to evaluate them and put all constraints aside.

STEP 5 Set out your criteria for a successful solution

Notice that we are doing this after generating ideas. We are less likely to be judgmental about ideas if we haven't got fixed criteria.

STEP 6 Rank and weight your criteria

Not all the criteria will be equally important, so sort out those that must be met and those that are not essential.

STEP 7 Evaluate the solutions

Start weighing up the solutions that you've generated. This is a fairly analytical process, but there are a few ways in which to do it. Two mistakes that people often make at this stage are:

- Throwing ideas out too soon, without even measuring them against the criteria, because they sound fanciful, or 'don't feel right'. You may need to justify why you didn't choose certain options.
- Choosing a solution by gut feeling and manipulating the criteria to fit. This shows that you haven't thought hard enough about your criteria. For example, if you choose an option because: 'I feel most people will like it, even though it costs more than agreed,' 'most people liking it' should have been a highly rated criterion. If it wasn't, it should not be the main reason for choosing a solution.

STEP 8 Decide

This may not be easy. Yes, you've been through the process and your option is the best, but you've now got to discard the others.

STEP 9 Put the solution into practice

Depending on the size and nature of the problem, you may need an action plan, target dates for the different stages and so on.

STEP 10 Monitor and review progress

Sometimes this will be a big project in itself. But even if your decision was simple, if you want to keep your brain fit, it's a great idea to spend some time reviewing your thought processes.

What have you learned?
What did you do well?
What would you do differently another time?

Implementability – How to give your solution a chance of working

Have you ever spent ages working on a problem, come up with what you really believe to be an excellent solution and made your presentation, only to have the thing gather dust on a shelf because no one's acted on it?

Perhaps you didn't put enough 'implementability' criteria into your decision-making process.

WHAT ARE IMPLEMENTABILITY CRITERIA?

These are the conditions that you and other people in your workplace will apply to any proposal. If it doesn't meet enough of them, it's just not going to happen:

- Is it politically acceptable? Is it going to go against the interests of anyone powerful enough to stop it?
- Is it organizationally consistent? Does it fit in with our usual practices, match the 'way we do things in this company'?
- Is it administratively convenient? Will the people who are actually going to be doing the work be able to?
- Is it relevant? Is the original problem important enough to the people who'll be making the final decision?
- Is it critical? Is this something on which the company gets judged?
- Is it technically feasible? The solution must look as though it will actually work.

Case Study

Martin was keen to organize the remodelling of the marketing office that he shared with eight other marketing people and Jan, who was the personal secretary of Bill, the head of the department.

Twice, Martin had drawn up plans, showing how everyone would have more space when the new furniture arrived and Jan would be nearer the door, so making access easier for Bill.

Each time, Bill looked at Martin's proposals and said, 'Great, I'll run it past everyone at the next meeting.' Twice, nothing had happened.

Finally, Martin lost patience and challenged Bill, 'Look, why does nothing keep happening? You agreed we needed to make that office look smarter.'

'Yes, but you didn't ask Jan what would be best for her. You've assumed she wants to be nearer the door. In fact, she doesn't want to leave the window – she reckons she's got the best view of the river in the whole building – better even than the Chairman. If Jan's not happy, I won't be.'

Martin had omitted to look at the implementabilty criteria for everyone involved in his reorganization.

Activity

1 Identify something that you are having trouble getting agreement on, or a problem you're having in getting a proposal accepted.
2 Compile a list of the people or groups involved in or affected by your idea.
   Don't forget all those who might lose out in some way if your idea went ahead.
3 Alongside each name, note the 'implementabilty' criteria that they will be using to judge your idea.
4 Then list all the ways in which your idea does and doesn't match.
   Don't forget to check that any assumptions you might be making are, in fact, correct.

OTHERS AFFECTED BY MY IDEA	THEIR IMPLEMENTABILITY CRITERIA	MISMATCH/MATCH

The whole person model for problem-solving

We found out earlier that our personalities affect our thinking. Although Jung suggested that we have preferences for Sensing or INtuition, Thinking or Feeling, we are all able to use our less preferred aspects and bring them into play when we are thinking about problems.

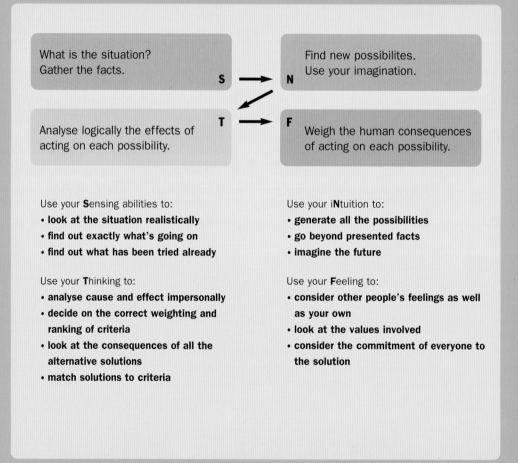

What is the situation?
Gather the facts.

S ⟶ **N**

Find new possibilites.
Use your imagination.

T ⟶ **F**

Analyse logically the effects of acting on each possibility.

Weigh the human consequences of acting on each possibility.

Use your **S**ensing abilities to:
- **look at the situation realistically**
- **find out exactly what's going on**
- **find out what has been tried already**

Use your **T**hinking to:
- **analyse cause and effect impersonally**
- **decide on the correct weighting and ranking of criteria**
- **look at the consequences of all the alternative solutions**
- **match solutions to criteria**

Use your i**N**tuition to:
- **generate all the possibilities**
- **go beyond presented facts**
- **imagine the future**

Use your **F**eeling to:
- **consider other people's feelings as well as your own**
- **look at the values involved**
- **consider the commitment of everyone to the solution**

CREATING A THINKING CLIMATE

A thinking 'climate' is as vital as a good physical environment. Nancy Kline, founder of 'Time To Think', works with organizations and people – helping them to think positively and creatively and reach better decisions. She has developed the 'thinking environment':

1 Attention
Listening with respect, interest and fascination

2 Incisive questions
Removing the assumptions that limit ideas

3 Equality
Treating each other as thinking peers
Giving equal turns and attention
Keeping agreements and boundaries

4 Appreciation
Practising a 5:1 ratio of appreciation to criticism

5 Ease
Offering freedom from rush or urgency

6 Encouragement
Moving beyond competition with each other

7 Feelings
Allowing sufficient emotional release to restore thinking

8 Information
Providing a full and accurate picture of reality

9 Place
Creating a physical environment that says to people, 'You matter'

10 Diversity
Adding quality because of the differences between us

APPLYING THE TEN COMPONENTS IN THE WORKPLACE

The ten components of the 'thinking environment' are quite simple – but, as the case study below demonstrates, not necessarily easy.

Case Study

The meeting starts on time and the chairman, George, settles everyone down and gets started on the first item on the agenda. He reminds everyone that the meeting must finish in three hours because the room's booked then for a focus group.

Two of the people in the room are having difficulty seeing because of strong sunlight coming through a window, but they don't say anything as they don't want to make a fuss.

Most people don't have anything to contribute for the first three items on the agenda, so those are dealt with quickly. Then, at item 4, everyone starts talking at once. George calls for order and tells Fred to keep quiet because we all know he has strong feelings about this issue and he should keep them to himself.

Eventually, an agreement is reached about an action point, but not before Mary and John have both managed to find something critical to say about every suggestion.

Tom has noticed that some of the figures in the notes are wrong anyway, but can't quite bring himself to mention it at this late stage of the meeting. Luckily, at this moment a tray of tea and coffee is brought in and everyone can focus on getting their drinks while Bill drones on about an idea he's had for improving the quality of meetings.

Does this sound familiar? Perhaps it's a bit of an exaggeration, although many meetings do seem to be like that. **Whose fault is it?** We often blame the chairperson, the people who hijacked the discussion or the fact that no one got the documents in time.

In the scenario above, it's fairly obvious that none of the ten components for a thinking environment was present. Do you think the people at that meeting would have been producing their best-quality ideas? Assuming they managed to agree on any actions at all, what do you think the quality would have been?

Taking responsibility

In fact, we could all take some responsibility for creating a thinking environment in our workplace. Just altering a couple of the components would make a big difference. Imagine how much better you'd be able to think if you knew you weren't going to be interrupted or hurried along.

THINKING ENVIRONMENT AUDIT

Think of one of your typical work situations. It could be a meeting, formal or informal, an appraisal session with one of your staff or your manager or a discussion with colleagues about a new system – anything that seems relevant and useful to you.

1 Look again at the ten components on page 61 and identify any that are already present in the situation. For example, 'Equality: We all get a turn to speak at our weekly project meeting and are encouraged to say how the project's going for us.'

2 Identify any that are not present. For example, 'Encouragement: We all seem to want to outdo each other moaning about how tough it is. We don't really listen.'

3 Think what you can do to remedy this. Aim for an action that you will feel able to take to allow that component to happen. For example, 'Next meeting I'll ask my colleague to say a bit more about their experience and not jump in with mine.'

How productive are the meetings you attend?

Does everyone leave the meeting with a sense of achievement?

What could you do to create a better thinking environment?

Motivation matters

People who are inspired to think and work in ways that produce the best results will be tapping into their own motivational forces.

Motivational theories start with the assumption that, given the chance and the right stimuli, people work well and positively.

The management psychologist, A H Maslow, suggests that these stimuli can be grouped into five areas:

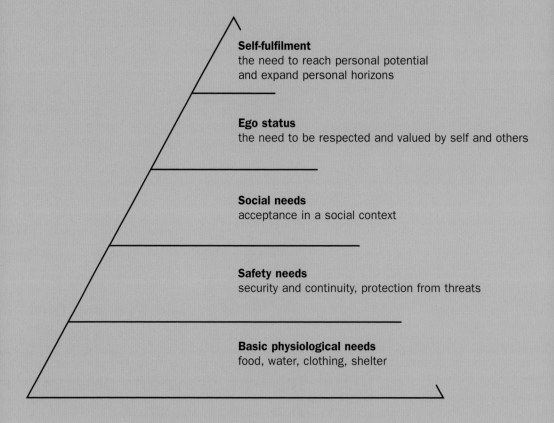

Self-fulfilment
the need to reach personal potential
and expand personal horizons

Ego status
the need to be respected and valued by self and others

Social needs
acceptance in a social context

Safety needs
security and continuity, protection from threats

Basic physiological needs
food, water, clothing, shelter

We will find it hard to operate at each higher level unless we have met the needs of the one below. And of course, our needs change throughout our working life.

You may have been very motivated by the sports facilities (allowing your social needs to be met) when you started work, but now with children to think about, your needs may have changed. Now, 'acceptance' means something different – perhaps an acknowledgment that you are still committed to your job, even though you can't join in sports events after work.

Given the chance and the right stimuli, people work well and positively

Employers and managers have to recognize that people's needs do change over time, and that each individual's needs are different. This is important if you are a manager.

Suppose your company is planning to move its head office across the country to the same town as its main production facility. Everyone has been assured that this is not a cost-cutting exercise with redundancies to follow. You think this is an exciting opportunity for you and your partner to move out of your flat into a house. Most of your team are also keen for different reasons. But one person is very concerned. They've just spent a difficult few months getting their elderly mother into a suitable retirement home nearby. They don't want to give up this job, and travelling back every weekend will be too expensive.

Think how demotivated they are likely to be – and the effect of this on their ability to think clearly about their work. It won't be of any help to them if you just say, 'Come on, just have a positive mental attitude.'

Using what we've done so far in this chapter, what could you do to help this person?

a) as their manager
b) as their colleague

For example, how would you help them to clarify the actual problem, and generate solutions?

Getting your thinking objectives clear

We've already looked at making sure we're thinking about the right problem and how to avoid limiting our thinking by assuming that we know what the solution is.

We do, however, need to make sure that we're heading in the right general direction. It would be a waste of time taking part in a working party to devise a new strategy for improving customer service only to discover that another group was working on reducing customer contact time.

When you have an appraisal or annual review, you probably set your objectives for the next year. You may find the acronym **SMART** useful when setting these objectives, to make sure they are:

Specific   **M**easurable   **A**greed   **R**ealistic   **T**ime-limited

In contrast, your 'thinking objectives' also need to be **CRISP**:

Constructive	Avoid negative, limiting language
Rough direction	Provide a framework rather than tramlines
Involving	Something worth working on
Suitable	In line with business and work objectives
Principled	Fit in with your values

If you have ever found yourself feeling rather half-hearted about something, not really wanting to take part, it maybe that the objective wasn't **CRISP** enough. For example, 'Come up with a strategy for improving service to telephone customers, while not increasing contact time' would be a **CRISP** objective.

On the other hand, 'Come up with a way of cutting the time we spend with each customer, without them knowing what we're up to' is not a **CRISP** objective as it implies some dishonesty and 'cutting' sounds more negative than 'improving'.

Activity: Motivation Check

1 Think of a time when you felt demotivated at work.
  What was it about the situation, those around you and
  you yourself that contributed to your demotivation?
  Which of your needs was not being met?
  How **CRISP** were your objectives?

2 Now, think of a time when you felt highly motivated at work.
  What was it about the situation, those around you and
  you yourself that contributed to your motivation?
  Where were you on the list of needs?
  Did you have **CRISP** objectives to help you?

3 Think about how motivated you are now at work.
  What could you do to raise your motivation if necessary and maintain it?

HOW TO REVIVE FLAGGING MOTIVATION

1 Have a break. You will return to the task feeling refreshed. A
  change of environment will help. You could also try some exercise.

2 Give yourself a pat on the back. Look back over what you've done
  so far and make yourself notice all the good points.

3 Give yourself a tangible reward – something that will improve your
  mood, and not induce guilt. An extra portion of chips might not be
  a good reward, but promising yourself a candlelit bath might be.

4 Find a way to break up what you're doing into chunks. If you
  already have, find a different way. For example, if you are writing
  a report, try breaking it into blocks of a certain number of words.

5 Try some creative thinking. How is your task like sailing a ship,
  for example? How would you be working a hundred years ago?

6 MAXIMIZE YOUR MEMORY

Everything we do involves our memories. We cannot think without accessing our memory and all the unconscious things we do, like walking or holding a cup, rely on the memory of how we did it last time. And yet many people believe that they have a poor memory. For example, the woman who leaves her umbrella on the train will be irritated with herself for her forgetfulness, yet as an accountant she works with huge amounts of financial information all day. The man who forgets to pick up the dry cleaning will give himself a hard time about his bad memory – despite the fact that he's a teacher.

In reality, we all cope with huge amounts of **new information** and perform amazing memory functions every day. In addition, because our brain capacity is so under-used, there's no reason why we shouldn't capitalize on it and increase our **memory powers**. As your memory improves, you'll begin to be able to process even more information, see the bigger picture and improve your confidence.

The trouble is, for many of us, using our memory is inextricably linked to stressful situations like exams or punishment at school for forgetting to do some homework. We may still get negative comments about our memory which simply reinforce our own self-critical view.

Your memory is better than you think

HOW MEMORY WORKS

There are two elements to our memory:
fixing something into the memory
recalling it when we need it again

These are, in fact, complex processes, that involve many parts of the brain working almost simultaneously.

When we sense something (hear a telephone number, smell a rose, touch a coffee cup and so on), an electrochemical pathway is laid down along the neurons from the site of the sense to the brain and across the synapses between them. The synapse is the minute gap between two neurons. There are 10 million billion possible connections, and each pathway is potentially a memory. The more a particular pathway is activated, the more likely it is that a memory will be created.

TYPES OF MEMORY

We have two sorts of memory – **explicit** and **implicit**.

The implicit memory uses well-worn neurological pathways to enable us to do familiar things time after time.

The **explicit** memory is for the things we have to remember consciously. For example, when you ring a restaurant to book a table, your **implicit** memory tells you how to use the telephone, and your **explicit** memory reminds you when you need to book for.

Feelings play an important part. We produce the chemicals adrenaline and noradrenaline when we undergo emotions and these act as transmitters. This partially explains why we are able to remember very clearly some things that happened at highly emotional times. So if you think about an achievement that you are particularly proud of, such as winning an award, you may well be able to remember very clearly what you were wearing, what the weather was like that day and the face of the first person you told. Unfortunately, of course, the same is true for memories associated with more negative emotions.

What happens when memory fails?

As emotion and stress increase, the adrenal glands work harder in order to get your body ready for its 'fight or flight' response, in whatever form that will take. The gland produces cortisol, which decreases the effectiveness of the neural connections, and so stops the memory working effectively.

This explains why we have more difficulty remembering the details of events when we were feeling panicky or highly emotional. Even Oscar-winners, well-used to public performances, report that they cannot remember what they said in their acceptance speech and that the actual ceremony is a blur.

'Everything happened so quickly, I can't remember much about it ...'

STUDYING MEMORY

Ironically, psychologists learn most about how memory works by studying people whose memories have stopped functioning properly, in the same way that an electrician can work out which way current is flowing in a complicated set of circuits when one bulb goes out.

Some conditions such as Parkinson's and Alzheimer's diseases are associated with chemical deficits, which mean that certain connections can no longer be made between neurons. Moreover, because we use different parts of the brain for different types of memory, people with such diseases, or who have lost part of their brain through accident, illness or surgery, may forget their name but can still play the violin. So the 'circuits' in the brain can be traced and studied.

Can we believe our memory?

Assuming that your memory hasn't been impaired by illness, injury or surgery, how much can you rely on it?

Activity

Imagine a coin or banknote. Draw both sides of it from memory in the space below.

Now get out the real thing. Have you remembered it well?

Of course, we don't need to carry an accurate description of a coin around in our heads because we can rely on the fact that we'll recognize one next time we see it. But what if we've witnessed a crime or an accident? Would we be reliable witnesses?

IT'S ALL RELATIVE

There are many factors that affect how we remember things. In one experiment, people were asked to draw a sketch map of their country with lines showing the relative distances between cities. In their own areas the lines were always too long, and the farther away on the map they went, the shorter they became relative to the correct length. Why? Were the participants exaggerating the relative importance of their own area, or did they simply feel more confident in their knowledge nearer to home?

Why do people have different memories of the same event?

Short-term memory

Up until the 1950s, scientists thought we just had one mechanism for memory. Everything went in and the brain stored as much as it could. Now we know that the brain uses several methods to remember information in different ways and for differing lengths of time.

Our short-term memories deal with two sorts of facts:
- **the trivia of life, such as the colour of shoes worn by the woman in the lift this morning**
- **the information we need for a brief period to carry out a specific task, but which then becomes irrelevant**

Try multiplying 39 by 8 in your head. You should get the answer of 312. Maybe you first multiplied 9 by 8 (72) and had to hold the 72 in your mind until you'd worked out 3 multiplied by 8 (24), which you then multiplied by 10 (240). Then you added the 72 (312). Once you'd got the answer, you could forget the 72.

Information from each sense is processed differently (see pages 16–17). This explains why we can do more than one task at once – as long as they don't need the same short-term memory pathways. For example, you can drive and talk to a passenger, but you will have difficulty talking to someone on the phone at the same time as speaking to someone at your desk.

HOW DOES THE SHORT-TERM MEMORY WORK?

The short-term memory has three distinct mechanisms:
- **the phonological loop, which handles sounds and words**
- **the visuo-spatial sketchpad, which registers images**
- **the central executive, which co-ordinates the others**

The phonological loop

The phonological loop works in two parts – a memory store and a rehearsal system. A speech-based memory trace survives for only a couple of seconds unless reinforced by the rehearsal system.

Try this experiment
Read each of the following sequences out loud. After reading each one, cover it up and recite it again from memory.
A hit, can, dog, toe, hit
B ban, hat, map, cat, ban
You probably found A easier than B, because sound is a factor and B had more similar-sounding words.

Now try these
C huge, big, great, wide, large
D old, late, cool, fat, good
Most people get similar results for C and D, showing that meaning does not have as much effect on short-term memory as sound.

Lastly, have a go at these
E opportunity, pneumonia, chancellor, refrigerator, organization
F hope, mumps, school, green, side
Here, the main factor is length, and you probably found E much harder than F.

Visual memory trace

Have you ever made a shape in the air with a sparkler or flashlamp? When you go to the cinema, what you're actually seeing is a series of still images, which you see as movement. Our brains hold each image for about one-tenth of a second.

The digit span

This is the first scientific test of short-term memory, devised in 1887. See how you get on.

Read aloud the first line of digits, once only, at the rate of about one digit a second. Then close your eyes and repeat the sequence. If you get it right, move down to the first line with five digits. Carry on doing this until you make a mistake. Continue until you reach a length at which you are always wrong. (If you need to, add extra lines of 11, 12 and so on at the bottom.)

8 3 1 9
6 9 2 7
4 8 5 1
9 3 4 1 7
6 8 2 5 9
3 7 1 8 6
8 6 5 1 4 9
2 7 1 8 9 4
4 3 8 1 7 2
7 5 8 6 9 4 3
5 2 1 9 8 3 7
1 7 5 8 6 4 2
2 7 5 4 6 3 9 8
9 6 3 7 5 2 1 4
7 2 9 1 5 3 4 6
6 8 3 2 5 9 4 7 1
4 1 9 7 3 8 2 5 6
8 4 2 1 6 5 9 7 3
9 4 1 7 4 6 5 2 3 8
7 3 4 2 9 1 7 6 8 5
3 8 1 9 5 4 1 7 6 2

Your 'span' is the longest sequence that you can recall. The average is six or seven digits. What this experiment shows is that time is the limiting factor. If you get to the end of the line before the memory of the first digit has faded, you'll probably remember the whole sequence. If you don't, you'll forget it. So, it follows that one way of improving your memory of numbers is to increase the speed at which you read them.

If you put the digits into groups of three and say them rhythmically, as a rap, this will help. So next time you want to remember a telephone number, just rap it a few times.

Long-term memory

We probably do remember much, much more than we recall. We think we've forgotten something: what was the name of our geography teacher all those years ago? We struggle to remember and then give up. Perhaps weeks later we come across an old photo of a school geography trip and the teacher's name pops into our mind. Context is very helpful to long-term memory.

We forget different things at different rates. Research has shown that our memory of names and faces declines fairly steadily over the first 30 years, with a rapid fall-off over the next 15 years. Academic learning suffers rapid early loss, but has much more robust long-term retention. The factors involved seem to be:

- **the vividness of the original experience**
- **the frequency with which we subsequently recall it**
- **our own ageing process**
- **'interference' – when the memory of a more recent event muddles or replaces the original memory. For example, even if you go to the theatre infrequently, you may have clear memories of your last visit a few months ago. If you go to the supermarket once a week, you may remember your last visit, but the rest will merge into one another and be a blur.**

As with our short-term memory, it appears that there is more than one process and mechanism involved.

Episodic memory

This is where we record **past events.** Most people remember very little from before the age of five and almost nothing from before they were three. This is probably because the brain is not mature enough to lay down specific memories, but may also have something to do with our language being undeveloped. Episodic memory is one of the most fragile and easily lost.

Semantic memory

This is where we store our **background knowledge** of the world. It reminds you what a car is and your best friend's name.

Episodic and semantic memories depend on each other but use different parts of the brain, which is why degenerative diseases may impair one and leave the other untouched.

TEST YOUR SEMANTIC MEMORY

In the list opposite, cover up the column of letters on the right. Read quickly through the names of countries. Cross out the ones whose capital cities you know immediately and those you are sure you don't know. Now concentrate on remembering the capital cities of the ones you think you ought to know but can't quite remember.

If you can't get them all, uncover the list of initial letters. That will probably jog your memory. (The answers are on page 139.) The feeling that something's on the tip of your tongue usually means that you do know it and all it takes is a trigger to release the memory. The trick is to find the right trigger and this is covered later in this chapter.

Country	
Norway	O
Turkey	A
Kenya	N
Uruguay	M
Tibet	L
Australia	C
Saudi Arabia	R
Romania	B
Bulgaria	S
South Korea	S
Syria	D
Cyprus	N
Sudan	K
Nicaragua	M
Ecuador	Q
Colombia	B
Thailand	B
Venezuela	C

Procedural memory

Our unconscious awareness of how to do things. It is the most durable memory process – even people with serious episodic memory loss may remember, for example, how to play the piano.

Prospective memory

The memory of things you have to do in the future. It is fairly fragile as it is least likely to be triggered by an accidental reminder.

Techniques for better recall

Motivation

We have looked at motivation in an earlier chapter, but it's worth reiterating here. How much you want and need to remember something plays a vital part in how willing you'll be to commit it to memory. However, just saying that something is important doesn't make it stick – the motivation is about how much effort you are prepared to put into the process.

So when you really want to remember something, try out some of the techniques in this section. Don't just hope it will happen.

How long it takes to learn something

Experiments have shown time and again that short bursts of activity help something to stick in the memory better and for longer. We may feel we know this from experience, when a last-minute 'cram' before an exam seemed to tell us more than all those weeks of sitting in a hot classroom. The trouble is, cramming isn't an activity that actually helps long-term recall on its own. Most of what you learned in a panic the night before will be gone as soon as the exam is over. Long-term recall needs short periods of high-quality activity.

If you have something to learn and remember, avoid sitting at it for hours – make a plan, do a part at a time and take breaks.

Physiological arousal or alertness

Our alertness is lowest when we are in deep sleep and highest when we are in panic or high stress. The optimum for most activity is in between, and may differ from one activity to another.

Work out when you are most comfortably alert. Things that don't need you to be thinking at your best can be done at other times – save this time for your most important thinking to ensure that what you need to remember goes into your long-term memory.

Early or late?

For a long time it was assumed that the best learning happens in the morning, and indeed most school timetables are still weighted in this way. Recent experiments threw doubt on this, though, when groups of schoolchildren were told stories in the morning and afternoon and then tested on what they remembered. The groups who had heard the story in the morning did better in immediate tests, but the groups who had heard the story in the afternoon did better in tests given several days later.

The following techniques work to improve various aspects of memory, and some may suit you better than others. Try to persevere with those that seem difficult at first; they are probably related to the aspects of your memory that you want to work with.

PATTERNS AND FRAMEWORKS – MNEMONICS

Rote learning really only works in a framework – our maths tables would be much harder to chant if 6 x 9 didn't follow right after 5 x 9. And frameworks and patterns reinforce the neurological pathways in our brains and so make the memories stronger. This fact leads to a range of techniques that can be very helpful when you need to remember details, facts, sequences and so on. A mnemonic is any device designed to help your memory. Once you get good at using them, they take a lot longer to describe than to put into practice. And remember, you are motivated.

A walk round the house

Probably the first person to use mnemonics was the Greek poet Simonides in the 6th century BC, and many people who perform amazing memory stunts today still use the method credited to him. This one is useful if you want to remember a list of things. You only have to do the initial work once, but you do need to spend some time on it so that it's well lodged in your memory. You can revisit it even when you don't have a list to remember.

Here's how it works

Conjure up a strong mental picture of your house, apartment or wherever you live. In your mind's eye, walk through it, stopping at ten places on your journey. Make as rich a picture as possible of each of the places. Stand and have a good look round in your mind. What colours do you see? What do you hear in each place? Don't worry if you don't have ten rooms, as long as you can identify ten separate locations.

Make sure you are clear about the route – you're going to use the same one every time you want to commit something to memory. Just to make sure, imagine yourself going back out of your house, going over your steps in reverse.

Now, suppose you want to remember ten things that you have to buy on your way home.

Imagine each item in its place in turn along your walk. Make the item memorable in some way. So you might put an enormous carrot doing a dance on the porch step, an immaculately neat pile of peas in the hall, a giant tomato tucked up in your bed, snoring loudly, or a bunch of bananas taking a shower in your bathroom.

Then, when you're at the market, take the mental walk round your house and all the items on your list will come readily to mind.

If you have fewer than ten things to remember, just go on part of the walk (but always start at the same point). If you have more than ten to commit to memory, just go round again.

You can also use this technique to remember important things about particular aspects of your work. For example, you could make the stairs the area that is always associated with your management activities. Then, whenever you need to remember something to do with your role as a manager, you imagine putting a picture of that thing on the wall of the staircase. When you've completed the activity, you can visualize yourself taking the picture down. In the same way, you can assign other work areas to other locations. Be as imaginative as you can – the more vivid the image, the better the memory trace.

Pegwords

This is a similar idea, but uses a list of ten memorable words, instead of places in your house, as 'pegs' on which to hang the things that you want to remember. What you do is think of ten words that rhyme with the numbers one to ten. Again, once you've got your list sorted, you'll use it a lot, so spend some time on this. It's best to have tangible nouns, rather than concepts or adjectives, because things are so much easier to visualize.

For example: one/sun; two/glue; three/tree; four/door; five/hive; six/bricks; seven/hen; eight/plate; nine/pine; ten/pen. (You can think of your own words if you prefer.)

Make your list as vivid as you can – you want it to stick. Then, when you have a list of items to remember, you associate each item with a number word. Make each image as ridiculous as you can – a rocket-shaped carrot zooming towards the sun, peas overflowing from a huge gluepot and so on.

Crazy headlines

The two previous techniques are mainly visual. Here's one that's verbal. It was designed by a 19th-century headmaster, Brayshaw, who wanted a way to help his pupils remember all the dates that history lessons of that era required. You can use it for any number, such as office security codes and PINs, and although it looks a bit daunting at first, it doesn't take long to master.

Brayshaw removed the vowels from the alphabet and set out a code for the digits from 1 to 0.

1	2	3	4	5	6	7	8	9	0
B	**D**	**G**	**J**	**L**	**M**	**P**	**R**	**T**	**W**
C	**F**	**H**	**K**	**S**	**N**	**Q**	**Z**	**V**	**X**

Office security code? Harry Doesn't Take Many Parrots: 32967
Bank PIN? My Mum is a Jumping Giraffe: 6643

Acronyms

This technique also uses initial letters, but this time you take the initial letters of the actual things you want to remember and make a word from them. We've already used at least two – **SMART** and **CRISP** objectives. An acronym doesn't have to be an actual word – a pronounceable nonsense word will do. 'ROYGBIV' is a good way of remembering the colours of the rainbow (red, orange, yellow, green, blue, indigo and violet). This technique can be used just as easily for remembering who attends which meeting, and who should get copies of the minutes. For example, if Anne, Bob, Henry, Steve and Tim attend the weekly budget meeting, you could remember them with the acronym BATHS.

Nonsense phrases

The initials can equally be used for words in a nonsense phrase. Another easy way to recall the rainbow's colours might be: 'Richard Of York Gave Battle In Vain', and you could remember who should be at the meeting with: 'All Bears Hate Squishy Tomatoes'.

Verbalization

As we've seen, the more vivid and engaging we can make an experience, the better we'll be able to remember it.

If you need to remember a sequence of events (the series of steps needed to process a customer application, for example), don't just read through the instructions a few times. When you have a go, talk it through to yourself out loud (or mutter). An even better way to help you remember is to teach someone else to do it or imagine that you are writing out a set of desk instructions for someone who is going to take over your work while you are away.

Remembering the names of people you meet

You meet someone, and you instantly forget their name. A person approaches you at a conference, and you can remember that you've seen them before, but what was their name? It's worse if they greet you by name. Like every other aspect of improving your memory, you have to want it to happen. Some people seem to be able to remember names without any effort, but in fact they will be using a method of memorizing names without realizing it.

Steps to improve your ability to remember people's names:

Step 1 Choose to respect this person by learning their name.
Step 2 Listen when you're given the name. It's so easy to focus on the handshake so their name doesn't register.
Step 3 Make sure that you hear their name properly.
Step 4 Imagine the name written down. Just doing this forces you to listen to it – many people are amazed to discover that they are suddenly good at remembering names just by doing this.
Step 5 Visualize the name. Perhaps it is like that of a famous person, or perhaps the surname is a profession or item you can use to make a visual image. Involve the person in the image.

Recalling 'hard-to-get-at' memories

Sometimes, a memory just doesn't seem to want to surface. Techniques used to help eyewitnesses in criminal investigations can also help in everyday situations, such as tracing a lost file.

1 **Recreate the original conditions in your mind.**
   How did you feel? What was the temperature like?
2 **Concentrate on the details, even if they seem unimportant.**
   If, in thinking your way around the route you took with the missing file, you notice a detail like a large plant, concentrate on that for a moment. It may bring other helpful images to mind.
3 **Visualize a remembered scene from another point of view.**
   Imagine you are outside looking in the window. What do you see?
4 **Replay a memory in reverse.**
   Visualize the room before you came into it. What happened before that ... and before that?

The memory gym

Here are some exercises and other things you can do to keep your memory in good shape.

Basic equipment – the physical components

If you're thinking that you like the sound of this gym more than the sort with the treadmills and weights – bad luck. Studies of the relationship between physical fitness and mental ability show that exercise can boost mental capacity by about 25 per cent. Even if you prefer not to do a lot of exercise, it's worth regularly checking your hearing and eyesight. A surprisingly high number of people overlook these basics.

Also, have a look at any medication you are taking. Of course, many conditions need regular drugs, but think about whether you have noticed any dulling of mental function while on a course of drugs. Sometimes it can be gradual, and it might be worth talking to your doctor about changing a prescription. Don't take any action concerning drug treatments without talking to your doctor.

Gentle warm-up

Sit comfortably and bring to mind your 'walk round the house' or 'pegwords'. Here's a shopping list of ten items. Use one of the recall tools above to learn them.

Biscuits
Washing powder
Bananas
Potatoes
Postage stamps
Eggs
Juice
Cheese
Bread
String

Pay attention

- Make a conscious decision that you are going to remember things.
- When someone starts talking to you, make the effort to listen and turn off your own inner tapes.
- When you park your car in an unfamiliar place, look for a landmark.
- When you take a new route, look out for things that you will be able to recognize on the way back, remembering they'll be on the other side then and will look slightly different.
- When you watch a film or read a book, make a conscious effort to notice key points and take the time at the end to recall them.

Another list

This time, make up a sentence with words beginning with the initial letters of the sun and planets.

Sun

Mercury

Venus

Earth

Mars

Jupiter

Saturn

Uranus

Neptune

Pluto

What were the items on the shopping list, again?

Be a child again

Before you went to school and began to get tense about your memory, you didn't have any hang-ups about whether there was a right or wrong way to learn to do things. Aim to do at least one of these childlike things every day:

- **use all of your senses and ask lots of questions**
- **stay positive and enthusiastic**
- **get engrossed in something**
- **try lots of ways of doing something, even if the first way works**
- **let your imagination run free**

More to remember

Learn this list of budget codes (try using crazy headlines):

Travel expenses	69421
Hotel accommodation	69437
Stationery	48115
Books and periodicals	47218
Boardroom hospitality	68226
Flowers and plants	68905

Write out the list of planets and the shopping list again.

Carry first aid

Don't be embarrassed about using your organizer, alarm clock, diary, tape recorder or even a humble notebook. Writing down a number, name or list can free your mind to think of something else. You do need to remember to use these aids consistently, though, and keep them handy. Don't forget that another person can be a very useful memory aid – sharing information and even getting them to remind you about certain things. Their memory might be strong in different ways to yours and this in itself might lead to all sorts of creative possibilities.

Lists again

How many of the countries and their capital cities from page 76 can you remember?

Now write out the other three lists you have been learning.

REVIEW

It would be a shame to waste all that motivation by failing to review your memory and finding it empty at the crucial moment. If you'd spent a lot of money planting your garden, you wouldn't expect to be able to leave it alone for weeks, or even days, and to come back to find it still in good condition. Get into the habit of going over things that you know you need to remember.

7 DEALING WITH STRESS

We tend to equate stress with overwork, being too rushed and having a lot on our plates. In fact, not having enough to do can also lead to stress and its associated symptoms because we need a certain amount of stress to function effectively. Strictly speaking, the definition of stress is neutral: 'the system of forces applied to a structure'. Without the right amount of stress, a structure such as a bridge would either collapse or explode – the stress keeps it together.

WHAT IS STRESS?

In human terms, stress has been described as 'unpleasant over- or understimulation'. The word 'unpleasant' is important here because each of us has a level of optimum stress at which we are able to perform effectively and, when things are going well, a certain amount of extra challenge can even be invigorating. For example, if you are in a job that depends on the needs of customers, you're likely to feel all right as long as customers present themselves in a steady stream, and you are able to deal with their requests. But you'll probably feel stressed if there aren't any customers or if there are just too many to deal with in the time you have available, although the stress may present itself in different ways.

How does stress manifest itself?

Stress shows itself in various ways: physical symptoms, emotional signals and changes in our behaviour. The easiest signs to spot are the physical ones like:

- **headaches**
- **upset stomach**
- **palpitations**

- **skin complaints**
- **neck and back pain**

  But we often disregard these, or associate them with some cause other than stress.

THE THREE LEVELS OF STRESS AND HOW THEY AFFECT OUR PERFORMANCE

1 NOT ENOUGH GOING ON: 'UNDER STRESS'

Feelings: bored
demotivated
restless
lethargic

Performance: distracted easily
keep putting things off
get preoccupied with
   unimportant details
low production

2 THE RIGHT AMOUNT GOING ON: 'OPTIMUM STRESS'

Feelings: energy
excitement
confidence and optimism
motivation
high self-esteem

Performance: sound judgment
logical thinking
creative thinking
high production

3 TOO MUCH GOING ON: 'OVER STRESS'

Feelings: irritability
fatigue
overwhelmed
close to tears
loss of perspective

Performance: forgetfulness
lack of concentration
irrational decisions
poor communication

How stress affects our thinking

Many of us are aware that stress affects our ability to think – either for better or worse. Just after an accident, we seem to be able to see exactly what needs to be done and wonder afterwards how we coped. On the other hand, think of the first few panicky moments of an exam, when the questions seem to be written in a foreign language. Now scientists are beginning to explain this.

The production of adrenaline helps us physically in the short term. Our hearts beat up to five times faster, our blood vessels expand and our blood circulates faster. We're ready for action. But too much adrenaline and its associated hormone, cortisol, can have a negative effect on the brain.

Recent tests have shown that cortisol, in particular, may be associated with memory loss. Volunteers were given lists of words and asked to recall them after a short time. Some of the people had previously been put through stressful experiences. The people who simply had to remember the words, without the other tests, did better than the others and the women did better than the men. It looks as if women and men are affected differently by cortisol.

STRESS AND COMPETENCE

The higher up the competence ladder we go, the less effort we need to devote to thinking about what we're doing. It seems that when we are stressed, the unconscious thought pathways are blocked and we move down the ladder. We are more mechanical in what we do and more conscious of having to think about it.

In fact, we may think too much about what we're doing. We become like the tightrope walker with an attack of nerves, thinking about how far away the ground is. She would need someone to talk her through her moves so that she could safely get back.

The stress we cause ourselves

When we were children, we learned how the world worked by watching and listening to the people around us. They gave us a set of values that they believed would help us to get on in our lives. For example, 'It's a good thing to help other people, and people will like you if you're helpful.' I doubt if anyone would argue with that. The trouble is that our most strongly held beliefs and values can get out of perspective when we are stressed and drive us to behave in ways that are unhelpful to us, and give us even more stress.

STRESS QUESTIONNAIRE

Try this simple questionnaire to find out which, if any, of the five 'stress drivers' you have and how they affect you. Answer each question 'yes', 'no' or 'sometimes'.

A

Do you set yourself high standards and then get annoyed with yourself when you don't meet them?

Is it important for you to be right?

Do you feel annoyed or irritated by small messes such as a spot on your clothes, or discrepancies like an ornament or tool out of place or minor errors in a bit of work?

Do you hate to be interrupted?

Do you like to explain things in detail and precisely?

B

Do you do things (especially for others) that you don't really want to do?

Is it important for you to be liked?

Are you fairly easily persuaded?

Do you dislike being 'different'?

Do you dislike conflict?

C

Do you tend to do a lot of things at the same time?

Do you find yourself getting impatient with others?

Do you have a tendency to talk over others, or finish their sentences for them?

Do you like to 'get on with the job' rather than talk about it?

Do you set unrealistic time limits (especially too short)?

D

Do you hide or control your feelings?

Are you reluctant to ask for help?

Do you tend to put yourself (or find yourself) in the position of being depended upon?

Do you tend not to realize how tired, or hungry, or ill you are, but instead 'keep going'?

Do you prefer to do things on your own?

E

Do you hate 'giving up' or 'giving in', always hoping that this time it will work?

Do you have a tendency to start things and not to finish them?

Do you compare your performance with others' and feel inferior or superior?

Do you find yourself going round in circles with a problem, feeling stuck?

Do you have the tendency to be the 'rebel' or 'odd one out' in a group?

Scoring

Score 1 point for 'yes', ½ a point for 'sometimes' and 0 for 'no'. Add up your score for each of the five sections, which relate to the stress drivers below.

Question	Score	Driver
A		'Be perfect' driver
B		'Please' driver
C		'Hurry up' driver
D		'Be strong' driver
E		'Try hard' driver

A score of three or more in any section indicates a tendency to that driver. Most people experience all of them at different times, but generally have two or three drivers that crop up regularly.

THE VALUES UNDERPINNING THE FIVE DRIVERS

VALUES	LEAD TO UNHELPFUL MESSAGES	WHICH RESULT IN THE DRIVERS
Achievement, autonomy, success, being right	Don't: make a mistake, take risks, be natural or childlike	Be perfect
Consideration, kindness, service	Don't: be assertive, important, different or say 'no'	Please
Speed, efficiency, responsiveness	Don't: take too long, relax or waste time	Hurry up
Courage, strength, reliability	Don't: show your feelings, give in or ask for help	Be strong
Persistence, patience, determination	Keep trying, don't be satisfied, don't relax	Try hard

Remember that it's not the values themselves that cause our stress problems – it's when we let those values get out of perspective. For instance, if you're just about to leave work and notice that there are too many spaces in the heading on your report, and you have to run for the train because you couldn't leave until you'd edited it, your 'be perfect' driver is having a negative effect on your stress.

HOW THE DRIVERS CAN AFFECT US

'Be perfect' Becky

She speaks in completed sentences, often numbering off various points. Her clothes are very co-ordinated and elegant. She is known for her high standards. She is good at focusing on the work in hand and always sees the best way of completing a task.

Becky gets stressed by anything she sees as other people's 'low' standards or illogicality. As her stress levels increase, she becomes more and more single-minded, seeing only her own point of view and becoming blind to other people's.

'Please' Pete

Pete loves to spend time with other people and is usually the first to break the ice at a social gathering. He feels responsible for those around him and tries to be pleasant and helpful to everyone.

Pete gets stressed when he's criticized, as he then feels as though everyone has misunderstood him. As his stress increases, Pete gets emotional and upset that people have ignored his work.

'Hurry up' Harjinder

Harjinder uses lots of phrases like: 'quick', 'get going', 'hurry up', 'don't waste time', 'there's no time to ...'. He often speaks rapidly, and will be doing more than one thing at a time, enthusiastically.

Harjinder gets stressed by silence and hates having nothing to do. He becomes impatient and interrupts people, and he'll arrive late for things as he tries to fit extra jobs in before he leaves.

'Be strong' Suzie

Suzie is good at working on her own, calmly and steadily, even under pressure. Her voice and body language give little away.

Suzie gets stressed when she has to ask for help. As her stress increases, Suzy withdraws even further into herself and becomes less able to deal with changes to her routine.

'Try hard' Tony

Tony uses the word 'try' a lot: 'I'm happy to give it a try', 'Yes, I'll try to get it finished'. In fact, he's often the first to volunteer.

Tony gets stressed when he thinks people will criticize him for not doing enough. He makes a lot of promises about tasks he's going to take on, but never seems to finish anything.

You may recognize a bit of yourself in Becky, Pete, Harjinder, Suzie or Tony. If you do, go back to the questions you answered Yes or Sometimes to in the stress driver questionnaire. Ask yourself:

What would happen if I said 'No' to this question?
How would I feel if I said 'No' to this question?
What messages have I had in my life about this?
Are these messages really helpful to me now?

Relax and let go of your stress

These exercises and activities will help to release some of the tension we carry around with us when we're stressed. Build in a few daily periods of stress release. If you're saying, 'I haven't got time for that,' get out your 'to do' list now and add 'relaxation' to it. Like any other exercise, you'll need to practise. After a while, the exercises actually save you time as you will be more energetic and able to deal with whatever comes your way more effectively.

BREATHING

As odd as it sounds, just concentrating on your breathing for a few moments will help to reduce the stressful chatter in your mind. By focusing on your own breathing pattern, you're diverting a bit of brain capacity away from thinking about whatever is stressing you.

TAKE A TEN-SECOND HOLIDAY

You can do this at any time and in any place. Get into the habit of having several of these during the day.

- **If you are sitting, put your feet flat on the floor and your hands loosely in your lap. If you are standing, place your feet comfortably apart and let your arms hang by your sides.**
- **Breathe in slowly to the count of five. Make sure you fill your lungs and expand your abdomen as you breathe. Notice how your spine stretches slightly as you do this.**
- **Breathe out slowly to the count of five, keeping your spine slightly stretched.**
- **Bring your breathing back to normal and carry on with what you were doing.**

THE FIVE-MINUTE REST CURE

This is something you can do sitting at your desk or to help you sleep. You can even adapt it for when you are on a crowded bus.

Make sure you are as comfortable as possible. Uncross your legs and arms, and give your back as much support as possible. It will work best if you can close your eyes.

- **Do three rounds of breathing as in the ten-second holiday.**
- **Notice the sounds of your body and tune out sounds around you.**
- **Concentrate on each part of your body in turn, from head to toes. Imagine each part becoming warm and relaxed. Pay particular attention to your head, face, neck and hands.**
- **Keep your breathing slow and rhythmic as you move your attention through your body, matching the feeling of letting go to each out breath.**
- **When you've released the tension in your toes, take one more slow deep breath in and out. Open your eyes.**

If you have extra time, try tensing up the various parts of your body, then relaxing them. This gives an even more relaxed feeling.

MEDITATION

Here are some quick meditations to help you to achieve a state of 'calm alertness'. Before each one, use the ten-second holiday breathing technique. Sit comfortably, but without slumping.

Beautiful place
Mentally create a place where you can feel happy and peaceful. Make the picture as full as you can – notice the sounds and smells. See it from different angles. Make a special place for yourself in the picture – the most secluded seat or a particular tree to lean against, for example. Return here whenever you like.

Sounds
Just let yourself hear every sound around you and within yourself. Separate them out and notice their pitch, volume and quality.

The body vase

Imagine yourself as a you-shaped glass vase. You are full of a cloudy liquid. Imagine that you have taps on the ends of your fingers and toes and when you open them the liquid level slowly goes down as all the stress runs out of your body. Close the taps.

Picture a hole in the top of your head. A refreshing, sparkling, clear liquid is pouring in, filling you with calmness and strength. When your vase is full, close the hole. Open your eyes.

PHYSICAL EXERCISE

Some doctors are now saying that those of us who sit at any activity for lengthy periods need to take regular physical breaks:

Screensaver

If you spend a long time working at a computer, you'll know how tired and achy you become. Take a short break every hour.
- Close your eyes and relax your face. Keeping your fingers together, gently massage your forehead and move your fingers in circles around your eyes in one direction, then move the opposite way.
- Put your fingers on your forehead and gently rub your temples with your thumbs.
- Close your eyes and cup your hands over them. Count to 20.

The neck and shoulder workout

- Put your hands over your shoulders. As you breathe out, let your head fall back and slowly bring your fingers over your collarbones.
- Place your left hand on your right shoulder and gently squeeze and release it. Repeat down the arm. Repeat on the other side.
- Rest your hands on the top of your head. Gently pull your head down and hold. Notice the slight stretch in the back of your neck.
- Raise a shoulder and rotate it backwards. Repeat on the other side.

The leg stretch

Keep one foot flat on the floor. Gently raise the other a small way. Rotate your foot one way and then the other. Repeat with the other leg. Get up from your seat and walk at least ten paces.

8 CREATIVITY AT WORK

Once upon a time, creativity was assumed to be separate from everyday life, best left to artists and poets, certainly nothing to do with the 'real world' of science or business, where 'wacky' ideas were not welcome. Creativity, like intuition and inspiration, was something indefinable, and probably you were either born with it or you weren't. Yet science needs – and indeed makes – intuitive leaps, and businesses need innovation or they'll stagnate and fail.

WHERE DOES IT COME FROM?

Is creativity, like spontaneity, something that just happens? If so, how will we know when it will happen? What many people do know is that being summoned to a meeting room so that 'We can all have fun and bounce ideas around' is almost guaranteed to stop their creative juices flowing.

Two French mathematicians, Poincarré and Hadamard, were the first to give the creative process a structure:

Preparation
You try to solve a problem using normal means.

▶

Incubation
You get frustrated when these methods don't work, so you go off and do something else.

▶

Illumination
The answer appears in a flash.

▶

Verification
Reasoning takes over again as you assess whether or not the new idea is any good.

Current thinking about thinking

Until recently, people thought that there were two types of thinking that lead to creativity:

'convergent thinking' – this means drawing on all your resources to solve a problem
'divergent thinking' – this means solving a problem by seeing it in a different way

Some people appeared to be better at divergent thinking than others. Although we now know that it is a more complex issue, these two models are nevertheless helpful in looking at creative processes, as we'll see later.

THE WIDER VIEW

Howard Gardner, who identified many of the different 'intelligences' (see page 18), suggests taking a wider view, saying that there are many different ways to be creative, including verbal, visuo-spatial and so on. Other psychologists say it is simply a state of mind, a readiness and willingness to let creative ideas form.

Whatever view they take of it, most people now agree that we can learn to be more creative. Using the analogy of sport, some people are undoubtedly born with the potential to break the 100-metre sprint record, while the rest of us will never do it. But assuming basic good health, everyone can get a bit fitter, whether walking, running or in a wheelchair. So you may not be the person who comes up with the next 'big idea', but you can learn thinking techniques that will help you generate more ideas.

Businesses need creativity or they fail

IT'S A BRAINWAVE

Our brain transmits waves of electrical impulses at different speeds depending on what it's doing. Current research is looking at the 'state of flow' of these brain waves.

There are four states:
Beta is the fastest (about 13–25 cycles per second) – most of the time when we're awake.
Alpha (8–12 cycles per second) – our brain when having ideas.
Theta (4–7 cycles per second) – in the first part of sleep.
Delta (half a cycle per second) – when deeply asleep.

To do our best thinking, we would like our brains to be in the alpha state. So how can we reach it? Some people seem to do it easily, even accidentally, while others need to work at it. Relaxation techniques have been shown to slow brain waves down to the alpha state. So, if you adopt the ways of dealing with stress from the last chapter, it seems you will have more creative ideas.

LOOKING FOR ALTERNATIVE EXPLANATIONS

As we've seen, our minds are good at making connections, but this is not necessarily helpful if you're trying to be creative. As the brain tries to connect a new thought to what's known, patterns get set and it becomes harder to think differently. We've also become conditioned to the idea that there's always one 'right answer'. For example, participants on a training course may be asked to do an exercise and present their results. A very common question is 'Have we done this right?' when there is no one, right way.

We are so keen to get any idea, we settle for one that presents itself, especially if it fits with what we are expecting. This is why we get stuck with over-generalizations. It's also why comedians use unexpected outcomes to stories. The 'non-connectedness' jolts us out of our thinking pattern and raises a laugh.

Of course, time is important and we can't just go on and on thinking about an issue indefinitely – we have to call a halt at some point. But if we let ourselves carry on after the first 'OK' idea, we might get to a much better one.

What do you see?

One way of answering this question might be: 'Black lines on a white page.'

Let's change the question: **what might this be?**

List as many alternatives as you can. Some suggestions are on page 139.

Changing 'What do you see?' to 'What (or why) might this be?' can lead to creative thinking.

For example, 'The trouble with having school-leavers in the office is that they only do their set hours, then leave on the dot of five.'

What do you see?
Some school-leavers going home at five o'clock.

Why might this be?
- They have no commitment to the company.
- They are keen on out-of-work activities or are studying after work.
- They want to get out of office clothes as quickly as possible.
- They don't know that they are supposed to stay on after five.
- They don't like the office environment.

This simple technique can generate lots of ideas. If you were in charge of the career development of young people in your firm, you could look at ways to make sure they were aware of expectations, give them feedback about the impact of what they do, offer ways to make studying easier or find ways to improve the environment.

Try **'why might this be?'** questions on these scenarios. Keep going, even when you think you've got an 'obvious' answer.
- The car park is always full by the time I get here.
- The stationery cupboard is a mess.
- Fred is always late to meetings.

Where to use creativity at work

You can use it anywhere and everywhere. You don't need to say, 'I think I'll be creative now,' or schedule it into your diary (although you can if you want). Just remember that you have a brain capable of creative thought at any time and let your mind be open to the possibilities.

Here are some principles of creativity to bear in mind:

Creativity is there already – let it happen

Aim for relaxed attention

Build up – don't knock down

Challenge the 'givens'

Manage the process – structure provides freedom

Activity

Try some of the techniques on the following pages and you'll soon find that you are able to apply your creativity in all sorts of situations. Some of the techniques you can simply do as you are; others may need a bit of space or other resources. Don't hold back from getting what you need, though – the increased creativity will be worth it.

RANDOM WORD CONNECTIONS

1 When you want more ideas, use one of the following ways to get a random word.

- Choose a book at random from the shelf. Open it anywhere. Close your eyes and put your finger on the page. Open your eyes and see what word you have chosen.
- Put a newspaper on the table in front of you. Choose a number between 1 and 20. Open the paper at that page, count down that

number of lines and then that number of words from the start of that line to choose a word.

- Close your eyes for a second and use the first thing or word you see in your mind's eye.

2 **Then think about all the ways in which your word is connected to the thing you are struggling with.**

For example, suppose you are responsible for organizing a seminar for senior staff from all your organization's branches. You are doing well with your 'to do' list, but you want to make sure you've covered everything. Get a random word (say, for instance, that you opened a newspaper at a section on social services and got 'cares'). How could this word help you generate more ideas?

Cares: caring for delegates outside formal sessions

How can people contact me beforehand if they've got any concerns about timings, arrangements? ▶ What about people with special needs? ▶ Has the venue got accessible toilets?

If you get a word like 'it' or 'a', use the technique again to get a different word. Don't look down the page until you find a word you like, as this won't be random and may be too closely connected to your original thought process.

METAPHOR

This can be a powerful technique to help you look at a situation from a new angle. What you do is ask yourself, 'How is my situation like a ...?' You can look for metaphors in various places.

Choose a setting from last night's TV programmes: '**How is my situation like a police station, a coffee bar or a waiting room?**'

Use the hobbies of people you know: '**How is my situation like knitting a jumper, cooking or walking in the country?**'

Look at objects or situations outside the window: **'How is my situation like a tree, a traffic jam or a postal van?'**

Note: *You need only one metaphor each time – several are listed here to give you the idea.*

Then list as many similarities as you can between the thing you are thinking about and that metaphor. Next add the aspects of your situation that the list leads you to. But don't worry if you don't get any new ideas.

Here is an example of how to apply a metaphor to a situation:

How is organizing a conference like knitting a jumper?
- Needs a pattern (programme; people must know what's going on)
- Check size as going along (conference objectives clear?)
- Lots of skill (have I got all the skills? Where can I get help?)
- Wool gets tangled (hitches are only to be expected)
- Different pieces, come together only at end (obvious)
- Need to see if it fits (don't forget feedback forms for delegates)

This is also a great technique to use quietly when you want to be the person who adds something useful to a discussion. In your mind, come up with a metaphor, and use it to generate a further discussion point or idea. If you're sitting in a meeting and the others keep going round and round in circles in their discussion about who has which spaces in the car park, you think 'How is this like ... (take a quick look out of the window) a tree? Branches ▶ shelter for small birds ▶ shelter = security ▶ people leaving late at night worried about security.' ▶ You say 'How about we reserve the spaces near the building for people who work the late shift?'

What would your mother think?

For this one, you choose someone who you know a bit about (even if it's only what you've read about them in the papers). So it could be your mother, or a more famous person. Then you simply list all the things that this person might say and do if faced with your situation. Some of them might lead you to new, helpful ideas about your situation, others might not.

Activity

Have a go yourself. List as many ways as possible that organizing a conference is like a doctor's waiting room.

Choose your own metaphor and see if you can come up with even more ideas.

Back to that conference you're organizing.

How would William Shakespeare handle it?

- He'd write a play: remember to get speaker's notes in time to prepare handouts.
- Theatre in the round ... make sure people at the back will be able to see and hear ... get a view screen and microphones?

Memory cards

- Get hold of a pack of small blank index cards.
- On each one, write or draw an object, an animal, an activity, a sport or a famous person. Add your own categories.
- Then when you're short of an idea for one of the activities above, you can use your cards to jog your thinking.

REVERSE QUESTION

This can be helpful when you are generating solutions to a problem. Ask questions that reverse what you are trying to do such as, 'What would happen if we didn't ...?' Or 'What would it be like if we did the opposite ...?' For example, you have a backlog of orders and want to get staff to work late, ask the reverse question:
How could we make staff leave early?

ANSWERS TO REVERSE QUESTION	POSSIBLE NEW THOUGHTS
Make sure all work's finished before 5	Maybe a shorter lunch?
Remove kettles and refreshment machines after 5	Provide extra refreshments after 5
Turn off the heating/air-conditioning	Make the environment more comfortable

ANTI-CREATIVITY – WHY WE DON'T LET CREATIVITY HAPPEN

As you read the previous sections, you may have begun to think of some of your own situations in new ways, but at the same time, a little voice in your head was whispering, 'It will never work,' 'They tried that last year,' or 'It's all very well for her.' The same thing happens when we hear other people's ideas. It's as if the creative part of our brain is trying to get its own ideas heard (and other people's acknowledged) above a cacophony of moaners.

Try to notice when this happens and challenge these 'voices' with a counterargument of your own. Once you get the hang of challenging anti-creativity, you will get better at allowing creative ideas to flow. You will be contributing to a generally positive atmosphere in which creative thinking will flourish.

INTERNAL MOAN	CHALLENGE
It's impractical.	Let's look for parts of it that will work.
It's too expensive.	Is there part of it we could do more cheaply?
I'll be laughed at.	Many great ideas started off by being ridiculed.
It's risky.	What's the worst that can happen?
I'll lose face if my junior staff has the 'winning' idea.	Haven't they done well under my management? It will reflect well on me.
I can't accept that this new person has had a better idea than me.	I'm glad I work in a place where we're not stuck in a rut.
This new idea might make my work up to now useless.	My work has been a good foundation, and this idea hasn't come from nowhere.
I don't want anyone else to get the credit.	I can also get credit for supporting good ideas and finding ways to implement them.
No one 'upstairs' will listen.	Let's find appropriate ways to 'sell' our idea.
I don't like the person.	I may not like them, but I can respect their intelligence.

Instant inspiration

Try these if you need a quick boost to your creativity.

1 How many words?

Write the key word from your problem down and make as many words as you can using those letters. See what those new words help you to think of.

For example: CONFERENCE
cone   core   once   free   fence   fern   concern   none

Then pick up on any words that strike you:
Fence: security arrangements
Free: goody bags for delegates
Once: repeat popular workshop sessions

2 Draw a picture

It can be of the problem, or of your ideal solution or of any stage in between. Now imagine you are an art expert explaining its meaning to someone who knows nothing about it. You may find new insights that you hadn't thought of before.

3 Soundtrack

What song or piece of music would be most appropriate as backing music for your problem? Why?

4 Back to school

Imagine you have to explain your idea to a class of bright eight-year-olds. What visual aids will you use? What sort of questions will they ask?

5 Hold the front page

Write a newspaper headline that sums up your idea. Use whatever style you like – getting it into tabloid format is challenging but fun.

Generating ideas in groups

When you are in a group, all the same guidelines for creativity apply as when you are alone: the environment needs to be right and mental attitudes need to be positive. You also need to be aware of group dynamics and power play.

The five basic principles for group thinking:

1 No criticism or judgment while ideas are flowing
2 Freewheeling – thinking in any direction is welcome
3 Quantity of ideas is more important than quality
4 All ideas must be recorded
5 A period of incubation should be allowed

A SUCCESSFUL GROUP-THINKING SESSION NEEDS

Someone to run it

Get someone who's not involved in the issue. If you can't, choose someone who has some skills in chairing or facilitating. Don't choose the boss. The facilitator should stay in that role.

A clear purpose

Everyone present should know why they're there. Spend a few minutes at the start, hearing what everyone thinks the purpose is.

A clear time frame

People will feel more comfortable if they know what's going on. It's better to have, say, an hour now and time to come back than to imply that everyone's got to sit here until this thing's sorted.

A clear process

The facilitator gives everyone a rough outline of what will happen (either agreed beforehand with the promoter of the project or worked out on the day with the people involved). It is also important to set out the five basic principles (see opposite).

Procedures for running group sessions

1 Welcome everyone and make sure that they're all comfortable.
2 Explain your role, the five basic principles and that all participants are equal partners in the process.
3 Explain what will happen and how long has been set aside.
4 Check that everyone understands the purpose of the meeting. Write it up on a flipchart sheet.
5 Try one of the following to get as many solutions up as possible:
- Ask everyone to call ideas out. (You may need someone to help you write them up.) Make sure that you write exactly what they say.
- Put people in twos or threes to think of as many solutions as they can. They write them on the flip sheets around the room.
- Ask people to write ideas on sticky notes and stick them to flip sheets. Everyone then reads them to trigger more new ideas.
- If ideas start to dry up, try one of the creative techniques from earlier in the chapter. Do not let this part run on and on.
6 Take a refreshment break.
7 Go back to the original problem and check that no one wants to rephrase it. (Sometimes one of the ideas that have been generated makes the problem look a bit different.)
8 Do one other technique to pull out any more ideas. Put people into small groups and give each group a blank sheet of flip sheets and lots of pens. Ask them to draw a picture of the problem as they see it being solved and the stages gone through to get there.
9 Make sure that all the ideas are visible to everyone. Give everyone a coloured pen and ask them to walk around the room and mark the ideas they like, honestly. They put three stars by their favourite, two stars by their second favourite and one by their third.
10 Look at the ideas that have come out on top and write them on a new flipchart sheet.
11 This will probably be the final product of this session. You will need another session to look at ways to implement solutions.

9 COMMUNICATING YOUR IDEAS

As well as processing all the information coming in, our brains prepare the messages that will let other people know what we are thinking.

COMMUNICATIONS QUESTIONNAIRE

Read the statements and rate each one with the closest number to your response:

0: Completely disagree 1: Disagree a bit more than agree

2: Agree a bit more than disagree 3: Completely agree

1 I have a wide vocabulary and I use it.

2 I can usually find more than one way to say the same thing.

3 I feel confident discussing my ideas.

4 People say I am never lost for words.

5 I am aware of the 'jargon' of my own specialism, and of people I work with.

6 I have an interesting speaking voice.

7 I vary the speed at which I speak, depending on what I am talking about and how I feel about it.

8 I like the way I speak and I am proud of my accent, if I have one.

9 Other people do not have any trouble hearing me, even in a large group.

10 My tone of voice usually complements my actual words.

11 I feel comfortable about looking people in the eye when I am speaking.

12 I think body language communicates as much as words.

13 I think about what I will wear and how I look before a presentation.

14 I am aware of my own 'personal space' and that of other people.

15 I believe age, race, gender and size affect communication.

16 I choose the best time and place to talk about something serious.

17 I wait until I think the other person is likely to be in a receptive mood.

18 When I have something to tell a colleague, I choose whether to email, phone or speak face to face.

19 I use visual aids for presentations.

20 I spend as long thinking about the person I am dealing with as I do in preparing what I am going to say.

Now add up your scores.

WHAT YOUR SCORE MEANS

41 and above You think about what will help to make your communication a **success.** You are prepared to put some effort into it as you are aware that there's more to the message than mere words. You make a conscious effort to make sure that your words are backed up by your body language and tone of voice. People will find you believable and easy to understand.

Between 21 and 40 When your message is fairly straightforward, you will be **heard** and **understood.** You spend time thinking about what you'll say, so you may sometimes be surprised if people don't get the message straight away. You are aware that you may be giving unclear signals with your body language, so you may try to minimize it by choosing your words even more carefully.

Below 20 You feel a bit lacking in **confidence** when it comes to **expressing** yourself. People sometimes fail to grasp your point, or seem to misunderstand you, and this may add to your frustration. You're not always sure when to speak up, so sometimes you miss an opportunity to get heard. You think that if only people would listen properly to what you're saying, you are actually quite clear.

Following up

The questionnaire does, in fact, look at four vital areas of communication. Look at your score in each section to see where you are strongest. We then explore each type of communication in turn over the next few pages.

Questions 1–5	**Verbal Communication:**	Score ....
Questions 6–10	**Vocal Communication:**	Score ....
Questions 11–15	**Visual Communication:**	Score ....
Questions 16–20	**Preparation:**	Score ....

Types of communication

VERBAL COMMUNICATION

Many of us are conscious that we have different vocabularies for different parts of our lives. We learned as teenagers that some of the words we used with our peers were not acceptable at home, and vice versa. At work you may speak differently in a formal situation than in the coffee lounge. This is quite normal. The trick is to make sure that the words you use are appropriate to the message, the situation and the other person. For example, if you wanted to apologize for forgetting to post a letter, you wouldn't start off with, 'I regret to inform you ...', but, 'I'm sorry ...'.

VOCAL COMMUNICATION

Research shows that when we first speak to someone, only 7 per cent of the first impression we create comes from the words we use, while 38 per cent comes from the way that we speak. As we get to know the other person, these percentages change slightly, but the words are the least significant part.

Another name for vocal communication is 'paralanguage'. It's the aspects of language to do with the voice rather than the words.

tone	**pitch**	**fluency**	**volume**
speed	**pauses**	**accent**	

We express our feelings through paralanguage. If a colleague says, 'No, I'm fine, don't worry about me,' with a sigh and a downward inflection, we can guess that they are not 'fine' at all, especially if there are visual clues as well, like a shrug or averted eyes.

A certain tone, just attached to one word or phrase, can alter the whole meaning of a message. For example:

'This exciting opportunity ...' (said with a sneer)

'I love this job.' (said with a humourless laugh)

Controlling vocal communication

You can control all aspects of paralanguage. The trick is awareness of **how your voice sounds** and **its impact on others.**

For example, notice what happens to your voice when you're angry, excited or nervous. When you are talking to someone and you are aware that you feel one of these things, it can help to say. **So: 'I'm a bit nervous about saying this ...' will help your listener put your message into context and help you control your nerves.**

Once you have begun to notice what your voice does, use a positive internal cue to change it. Your inner voice saying, 'Keep your volume up,' will be more helpful than, 'Don't mumble.'

Keep your accent. Certainly don't apologize for it, or try to remove it. If you notice that particular words, phrases or intonations tend to get misheard or misunderstood, think about ways to vary them. And check it's your accent that's the issue – could it be your choice of words?

VISUAL COMMUNICATION

This is sometimes called 'body language', but it's more than that. It is the ways in which we communicate without words. It can account for about 55 per cent of a first impression, and around 50 per cent of any communication after that.

Types of visual communication include:
facial expression
eye contact
physical proximity and contact
gestures
posture
appearance

The main thing to remember about all types of visual communication is that they tend to be more easily believed than the verbal part. So if the visual communication matches the words, it will reinforce the message. But if it contradicts the words, it will be taken as the true meaning of the message.

Preparing to communicate

'When I am getting ready to reason with a person, I spend one third of my time thinking about myself and what I am going to say – and two thirds about the other person and what they are going to say.' Abraham Lincoln

You want to talk to someone about something that's been bugging you. To avoid a shouting match, you prepare what you want to say, and in fact you mentally devise a whole 'script'. 'I'll say this, then they'll say that, then I'll say...'. When you actually talk to them, it doesn't work out the way you'd planned. This is because the other person didn't get a copy of the script beforehand and you spent too long thinking about your viewpoint and not about theirs.

A similar thing happens in all sorts of situations:

In a seminar when the presenter uses too many slides because they've got a lot of information to impart. They haven't given a thought to the audience, some of whom know most of it already and all of whom have just had a good lunch.

When a manager who's heard that walking around to chat to staff is a good thing perches on your desk to tell you about a new directive from head office, totally disregarding the fact that you are obviously reading a lengthy document.

In each case, the message is good, important and interesting, and the person delivering it is pleasant, enthusiastic and good at their job. But unless they work harder at looking from the other person's point of view, they will have wasted their breath.

Real conversations don't follow a script

THE VIEW FROM YOUR HILLTOP

When you talk to someone else about a topic, it's fairly obvious that they will see it from a different viewpoint to you. It may be completely different or only slightly, but they are not you, so it will be different. The understanding gap is made wider because each of us is standing on a virtual hilltop made up of our own experience and background, feelings, values and beliefs.

If we want someone to be persuaded about our view, we have two options:
- **climb their hill**
- **get them to climb ours**

Climbing their hill will involve you asking questions like:

What experience have you had of this?

What do you feel about this?

What do you believe is the right way to do this?

Getting them up your hill will involve you telling them:

Your experience

How you feel

Your beliefs about it

The most persuasive communicators will do a bit of both, remembering that their own view at any stage may be different to the other person's.

Getting ideas across at meetings

It doesn't matter how brilliant your idea is, if you don't pitch it correctly and don't communicate it effectively, it won't happen. Careful preparation and how you behave and speak in the meeting will help your thoughts get a fair hearing.

Before the meeting

1 Make sure that you have everything you need.
2 Think about who'll be there: who will be your allies and who won't.
3 If possible, talk to the other people beforehand to canvass their views, check what they are going to say and share information.
4 Think about where you'll sit. Get there early and choose a good place where everyone will be able to see you. In a formal meeting, it's good to sit near the person chairing it. If you are allocated an inconvenient or uncomfortable seat, ask to move, or at least get the source of discomfort, such as bright sunlight, removed.

At the meeting

1 Speak up early in the meeting with a positive comment. If the chair asks for views, even if it's not particularly important that you contribute to this point, say, 'I agree with all that's been said so far.' This gets your voice into the air, and avoids it squeaking when your turn comes, and people will have a positive 'vibe' about you.
2 You may need to use a physical signal that you want to contribute – lean forward or briefly hold up your hand.
3 Take a breath before you speak.
4 Introduce yourself if some people don't know who you are, or you missed earlier introductions.
5 Start on a positive note. 'Derek's idea is interesting, although I disagree about the costings,' is more positive than starting with, 'I disagree ...'. Ensure that your positive note is true, or you'll sound insincere. Avoid clichés like the plague! Most people mistrust 'with respect' and interpret it as, 'I have no respect for you, you fool.'

6 Make sure that your verbal, vocal and visual messages match.
7 Keep eye contact appropriate and include everyone as you look around the room.
8 If you have a lot to say, break it up into manageable chunks and summarize as you go along. Make it clear what you are asking the people at the meeting to do and help the person making the notes by letting them know what you want recorded.

Other useful interventions in meetings

If you don't understand something – ask. The chances are that you'll be thanked later by others who didn't understand either.

If you notice that the discussion is going off the point or going over the same thing, say, 'I propose we move on.' Then it's open to anyone to make a counterproposal. But most will agree with you.

EXERCISES TO BUILD UP YOUR COMMUNICATION SKILLS

Verbal

1 Find a clearer way to say each of the following:
a) It would be much appreciated if you'd let me have your response by Friday.
b) We are in an ongoing staff shortage situation.
c) This activity will not be able to be implemented for some considerable time.
d) An adequate explanation for the delay was not forthcoming from the suppliers.
e) Alternative strategies for the realization of our objectives will have to be determined.

2 Which is the correct word to use in these sentences?
a) A referee should be *disinterested/uninterested* in the result.
b) This checkout is for six items or *fewer/less.*
c) Our new boss was *formally/formerly* in the pub trade.
d) How will the changes *effect/affect* you?
e) We have changed our *stationery/stationary* supplier.

3 Find a positive way of expressing each of the following ideas:

a) Three out of ten people can't operate the new system.

b) I disagree with most of what Sue says.

c) I'm hopeless at estimating how much paper we'll need.

d) It's no good talking to George when he's in a mood.

e) Everyone knows that's a stupid idea.

Vocal

1 See how altering the tone of your voice affects sound and meaning.

a) Read the following sentence out loud eight times, putting the emphasis on a different word each time.

The office has been painted green and white.

b) Now think of a feeling (anger, joy, sorrow or fear) and read the sentence with that feeling in mind.

c) Now read the sentence aloud in a monotone.

2 Read each of the following sentences aloud a) as if it's bad news, b) as if it's a question and c) as if it's an exciting discovery.

The photocopier has broken down again.

Tom wants a cheese sandwich for lunch.

We've just recruited an excellent new accountant.

Notice what happens to your tone, pitch, speed and volume.

Visual

1 Face a mirror. Say each of the following sentences aloud, trying to match appropriate gestures and facial expressions to the words.

a) I'm really pleased to meet you.

b) This is a huge problem.

c) I'm annoyed that you've arrived late again.

d) I'm rather embarrassed about mentioning your poor spelling.

e) It's my fault, I'm sorry.

Say them again, using gestures and facial expressions to convey an opposite (or different) message. Which did you find easiest and hardest. Which feelings are you most comfortable expressing?

2 Turn on a TV discussion programme with the sound down. Watch one participant's gestures, posture and facial expressions. What clues might these give about the person and what they are saying?

3 Next time you are in a public place with strangers, tune in to your inner voice and what it's telling you about the people you see.

What do you notice about people in the first split second? What does their age, race, size and gender make you think about them? This isn't about stereotyping – it's about noticing that we make these snap decisions and allowing ourselves to challenge them.

Non-verbal communication checklist:

Posture and distance

- Do you sit or stand upright or slouched?
- Are you too near to or too far from the other person?
- Are you higher or lower?

Eyes

- Is your gaze relaxed and friendly and do you maintain eye contact?
- What is your expression when people approach you?

Mouth

- Do you clench your jaw?
- Is your smile genuine – or misleading?

Voice

- Note your tone, inflection and volume.
- Do you whine or bellow, mumble or swallow your words?

Gestures

- What do you do when someone is approaching?
- Are your hands covering your mouth or fiddling with your hair, or clasped behind your back?
- Do you shift from one foot to the other?

Appearance

- What does your appearance say about you?
- Does it convey the impression that you want?

Breathing

- Noticing your breathing and learning to relax your body allows you to manage your feelings and communicate clearly.

CONCLUSION

This book has tried to give you some insights into how your brain works, when it is at its best – and when it's not working so well.

- You've identified your strengths and weaknesses, some of which you already knew, and some which may have surprised you.
- You have tried some techniques that have already begun to develop your brain's amazing potential.

No one suddenly becomes a great thinker simply by reading a book. **Practising** and **implementing** new ideas will mean changing the way you see things and maybe taking a few risks.

Clearly, a major factor in whether you continue to keep up the good work you've already started and make even more progress is the extent to which you are prepared to put it all into practice. Keeping your brain fit needs a good deal of **commitment** and a regular analysis of your performance.

CONTINUING SELF-ASSESSMENT

Make a learning diary

A learning diary is a great resource for recording your development. You can track your progress and reflect on the benefits that it is having for you and your work.

Reviewing what you've learned

Your first task is to look back over the chapters of this book and any notes you've made, and identify what you've learned or had confirmed about yourself so far. Then add a note about how this will be useful to you. Just aim for two or three key points in each section that strike you as you review.

REVIEW TABLE

TOPIC	WHAT I LEARNED OR HAD CONFIRMED	HOW I CAN USE THIS
How well do I use my senses? *(see pages 16–17)*		
How intelligent am I? *(see page 18)*		
What kind of thinker am I? *(see pages 25–28)*		
What's my learning style? *(see page 30)*		
What's my personality type? *(see page 32)*		
What competences do I have? *(see pages 38–40)*		
How do I use my time? *(see page 47)*		
What thinking blocks do I have? *(see pages 52–53)*		
How do I solve problems? *(see pages 54–57)*		
Do I operate in a 'thinking environment'? *(see page 61)*		
How motivated am I? *(see page 67)*		
Do I have CRISP objectives? *(see pages 66–67)*		
How well do I understand my short-term memory? *(see pages 72–74)*		
What techniques can I now use to improve my long-term memory? *(see pages 77–82)*		
What are my stress drivers? *(see pages 89–90)*		
How do I relax during my time at work? *(see pages 93–95)*		
What techniques can I use to boost my creativity? *(see pages 100–105)*		
How good are my communication skills? *(see pages 108–109)* verbal? vocal? visual?		

DEVELOPMENT PLAN

Now you need to make a plan to develop yourself. Remember, development isn't only about overcoming your weaknesses – it can also be about enhancing your strengths.

Look again through the list you've made. Choose a few areas that you particularly want to work on. Don't be too ambitious – three would be a realistic number of things to focus on the first time round.

For each one, answer these questions:

What words or phrases describe how, ideally, you'd like to be?

For example, 'I want to be the one who comes up with ideas in meetings.'

What four things will you have to do to achieve this?

a) Ask questions to make sure that I'm clear what we're talking about.

b) Put aside my fear of looking silly.

c) Listen fully to be able to build on others' ideas.

d) Try some instant creativity techniques.

Where or when do you find it difficult to do this at present?

When Jane is chairing the meeting, because she often seems to have her own ideas and not listen to anyone else.

What can you do to overcome this difficulty?

Talk to Jane about some group idea-generation techniques.

Who or what can help you?

I know Bill is also keen to have more creative meetings – he'll be an ally.

When will you try it?

I'll talk to Jane tomorrow, and then come up with some ideas at our strategy meeting on Tuesday.

If you are serious about development, it is worth writing your thoughts down. As you progress, you can look back over your notes and notice that things you once thought challenging are now becoming easier.

Put reviewing your learning diary onto your list of regular things to do. It will also be interesting to re-do some of the exercises and questionnaires in the book to see how you change as a result of putting the techniques into practice.

Your daily brain workout plan

Every day

Choose one activity in each category. Answers are on page 140.

Creativity and lateral thinking

◀ **1** How many ways can you think of to get the ball out, without damaging the ball, the tube or the floor?

2 Who would you choose to play you in a film of your life? Why?

3 If your organization was an animal, what would it be? Why?

4 What comes next in this sequence?
L 15 30 40 A ? ? ?

◀ **5** What could this be?

6 What would be the theme song for the TV series about your life?

7 Which is the odd one out? Why?
17 3 2 7 12 11

8 Think of as many ways as possible to reframe this problem: Everyone needs more time off work.

◀ **9** Complete this drawing in whatever way you choose.

10 Treat yourself to an intricate colouring book and some coloured pencils and spend half an hour colouring in.

Analytical and logical thinking

1 Fill in the missing number.

				?
				52
				42
				39
41	45	48	43

2 Find the missing word.

123	=	RAG
456	=	NET
726	=	SAT
7612435	=	?

3 Fill in the missing squares.

Zw6	Xy5	Yx3	Wz4
Wz5	Yx3	Xw4	Zy6
Yx3	Wz4	Zy6	Xw5
Xy4	Zw6		

4 Which shape?

A   B   C   D   E

?

5 Which of the following is not illustrated by this drawing?

End of a pencil   Cone
Wheel and axle   Wine glass
Long tube   Drawing pin
Salt cellar   Toffee apple
Spinning top   Circle with a dot in the middle

6 Convert this to numbers.

```
  K J H
  N M P
H I Q Q
```

7 How many ways are there to get from A to B by following the direction of the arrows?

8 I wrote four consecutive single numbers on four pieces of paper. Then I turned the papers over and wrote four consecutive single numbers on the back. On each piece of paper the two sides totalled 14. If my first four numbers add up to 30 and my second four add up to 26, what are the two numbers on each piece of paper?

9 Which piece fits the square so that all rows and columns add up to the same total?

10 Treat yourself to a logic puzzle magazine and try to solve one.

Sense Boosters

Sight	Look at an object and focus on the spaces and shadows around it.	Look at a colour picture in a newspaper or magazine. Focus on the colours rather than the subject of the picture and notice all the shades and patterns.
Hearing	Listen to some music of a type you don't normally listen to.	Close your eyes and listen to the sounds around you. Try to picture how far away each of the objects or people is from you.
Touch	Close your eyes, reach out and touch your desk lightly with the tips of your fingers and gently move them over various objects. Try to visualize what your fingers are telling you.	One by one, name all the things that are touching you at the present moment.
Taste	Look at a picture in a cookery book or magazine. Imagine the tastes of the different foods and where you would feel them on your tongue.	One by one, touch the tip of your thumb to each of your finger tips in turn. Notice how different each one of your fingers feels.
Smell	Close your eyes and try to notice all the smells that are around you. They may be faint, and you will have to concentrate.	Look at a picture in a cookery book or magazine. Imagine the smells of the different foods.

Memory Builders

1 Look at these items for two minutes.
Then cover them up and list or draw as many as you can.

2 Use your 'pegwords' (see page 80) or your 'walk around the house' (see page 79) to remember this list:

ball

cards

train

marbles

puzzle

skates

bricks

doll

chess

book

Cover it up and write it out from memory.

3 Study these for two minutes and cover them up. Draw as many as you can recall.

4 List as many as you can of the people you spoke to yesterday.

5 Use one of your memory tricks to learn this list:

Santiago	**Oslo**	**Warsaw**	**Rome**	**Washington**
Pretoria	**Wellington**	**Bangkok**	**Athens**	**Moscow**

Cover it up and write it out from memory.

6 Look at your desk for two minutes. List everything that is on it from memory.

7 Draw a sketch map of a route you are familiar with. Compare it to a map of the area.

8 Use one of your memory tricks to learn this list:

Shoe

Jacket

Blouse

Sock

Dress

Coat

Tie

Scarf

Skirt

Sweater

Cover the list up and write it out from memory.

9 Study these items for two minutes. Cover them up and list or draw them from memory.

10 Write the story of your first hour at work today.

At least once a week

Choose one activity from each group.

Where appropriate, the anwers are on page 141.

Polish up your linguistic intelligence

1 Complete the dishes:

_AS_ _ NE	GO_ _A_ _	_O _S_A _A
_ A _ _ L _	_ U _ _ Y	H_ _ _U _ _ _ R
_ M _LE _ _ E	R _ _ I _L _	_ N _ H _ _A_ _S

2 Fill in this minimalist crossword.

Across	Down
1. To surpass	**1. More than**
3. Written composition	**2. American city**

1	2
3	

3 What are:
- **a) Hyssop**
- **b) A teal**
- **c) Teak**
- **d) A borzoi**
- **e) Gouda**
- **f) An omnivore**
- **g) Lapis lazuli**
- **h) A plectrum**
- **i) Pimento**

4 Change HEAD to TAIL, altering one letter at a time.

HEAD

_ _ _ — _ _ _

— _ _ _

TAIL

5 Each pair of words has answers that rhyme.

a) GAME BIRD	**PEN REFILL**
b) HUMAN	**ENTRANCE**
c) YEARN FOR	**DIG FOR**
d) UNIT OF TIME	**SONG BIRD**
e) CULTIVATED AREA	**SET LIKE CONCRETE**
f) IMPOSING	**BRIDGED**

6 Add a different three-letter word to each list to make words.

a)	b)	c)
ST _ _ _	ST _ _ _	ST _ _ _
BR _ _ _	BER _ _ _	BR _ _ _
L _ _ _	L _ _ _	L _ _ _
M _ _ _	M _ _ _	H _ _ _
W _ _ _	CR _ _ _	W _ _ _
TH _ _ _	DON _ _ _	BL _ _ _

7 What are the plurals of these words?

Potato

Hoof

Reef

Deer

Ally

Alley

Journey

Child

Ox

Dance

Princess

Audience

8 The answers to these pairs of words are pairs that sound alike but are spelled differently. for example, FRUIT and TWO = PEAR and PAIR.

CARRY and NAKED

CREATED and FEMALE SERVANT

KNOTTED and EBB AND FLOW

HELP and ASSISTANT

LEND and SOLO

HOUR and HERB

SHEEP and TREE

NUMBER and CONSUMED

VERSE and FROST

DISCOVER and MADE TO PAY

9 Anagrams: all of these words can have their letters rearranged to make another real word.

THOUSAND

FIGHTER

LOVELY

INCLUDES

SUNLIGHT

TRANSIENCE

EDUCATION

PIECRUST

EARRING

HAPPIEST

INTRODUCE

DISPROVE

10 Synonyms: write a word in the brackets that means the same as the ones outside them.

CONTAINER (   ) FIGHT

BIRD (   ) NO SCORE

CARRY (   ) ANIMAL

CORRECT (   ) A HAND

TREE (   ) YEARN

LEVEL (   ) STAGE SCENERY

HEARTH (   ) IRRITATE

SHIP'S SPEED (   ) TIED ROPE

Tone up your mathematical intelligence

1 Thrifty Mrs Jones runs a hotel. She keeps all the little bits of soap that the guests leave behind and she can make a new bar from every nine bits. How many new bars of soap can she make from 729?

2 What's the missing number?

3 If 1000 books cost $68.90 how much would 340 cost?

4 Which is the odd one out?

5 When full, a barrel holds 75 litres of oil.
How many litres are left when 40 per cent has been used?

6 What is the missing number?

7 The cake machine ices five cakes every minute. How many cakes will be iced in 8 hours if the machine keeps working at the same rate?

8 A storage area measures 9m x 6m x 8m. How many boxes measuring 4m x 3m x 2m could you pack into it, assuming you had free access?

9 Which is larger – 25 per cent of 180 or one-third of 138?

Sharpen up your intelligences

Notice that the things you do every day are using your range of intelligences. Remind yourself which ones you are using at any one time. Be on the look-out for opportunities to develop the ones that you're less comfortable with:

Visual
Imagine that you're in a picture in the newspaper. What would you see from behind the subject? From above? From below?

Physical
Notice the space that you are occupying. Imagine an artist is going to make a sculpture of you and has filled the space between you and the walls with a moulding material. What does your statue look like?

Musical
Imagine that you're in an opera. If you can be private, sing a few lines to tell the audience what is going on. What instruments could accompany this scene?

Social
Look through your contact list. Ring someone you haven't spoken to recently.

Environmental
If you ran your organization, what measures would you introduce to improve the working environment? What could you do in real life?

Practical
Find something to take apart and put back together. Study its component parts as you do it, and try to get an understanding of how they work.

Emotional
Draw a picture of a thermometer. Plot your emotional state on it for a day.

Spiritual
Let your mind rest on a big issue that you feel is important in the world. If you wish, find someone you feel comfortable with and talk about this issue.

Balancing your life for a fitter, healthier brain

The phrase 'work–life balance' was almost unheard of ten years ago. We have moved on from the concept of 'juggling' career and family to 'balancing', which in theory sounds slightly more restful. In practice, of course, many people are still struggling to deal with all the demands on their time, and in some organizations, flexible working is still equated with lack of commitment.

Some of the benefits of technology have also given rise to changes in work patterns and customer expectations that throw the concept of work–life balance into disarray:

- The speed of communication means that we are getting used to instant responses. We complain if we have to wait for supplies or services, and this puts stress onto those who provide them.
- Mobile phones mean that we need never be out of reach.
- Emails give a sense of urgency to messages that once would have waited in an in-tray without the organization grinding to a halt.

For many people, the boundary between home and work life is no longer clear, as more people use technology to work from home for some, if not all, of the working week. This may save on the stress of daily commuting, but adds pressure as people take on extra work to fill that 'extra' time and work harder to convince the organization that they are actually working.

Most of us are well aware what is happening to us. The old saying goes, 'No one lies on their death-bed and says, "I wish I'd spent more time at work",' and have you heard the one about the graveyard being full of 'indispensable' people? Even if they are rather morbid, these comments show that we do see the connection between overwork and ill health, at the least.

Here are some questions to ask yourself:

Do I work longer hours than I used to?

Do I work longer hours than I need to?

Am I achieving something important when I stay late at work, or am I just keeping busy?

Do I feel guilty if I leave the office before anyone else, or arrive later than them?

Activity

Try this exercise to identify what you could do about getting your life more in balance.

In the first circle, draw segments that roughly represent the amount of time you give to each area of your life. It's not a scientific survey, so you don't need to work out hours and minutes, but simply get a general idea.

Then, in the second circle, draw the segments as you'd like them to be. Don't be constrained by reality – go for what you want.

 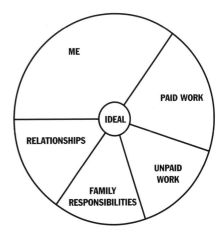

Which area has increased?

Which has decreased?

What would have to happen in real life for this change to take place?

Healthy living

You probably know about the benefits of a healthy diet and regular exercise. You may even put the principles into practice. Just in case you don't, here are some pointers.

DRINKING

Drink plenty of water every day, at least two litres (4½ US pints). Most people live in a permanent state of partial dehydration, which means that their brains function at less than full capacity and their bodies take longer to dispose of waste products. Recent studies have shown that children who drink eight glasses of water a day do best in test results.

Alcohol
Although there is a lot of water in beer, this isn't a reason to drink lots of it, or any other alcoholic drink. For some of us, alcohol causes us to be less inhibited and so may improve our creativity, but as alcohol is a depressant, it also reduces the flow of blood to the brain and so reduces thinking power.

Caffeine
Caffeine is a stimulant and has the effect of increasing alertness in the short term, but, as it is a diuretic, it also leads to dehydration. You should drink two glasses of water for every cup of coffee you have.

Most people live in a permanent state of partial dehydration

EATING

We need a balanced diet. Our mothers told us this, and the only thing that has changed over the years is that experts now have a different idea about what constitutes a balanced diet. Diet is another area where innovation has not always led to improvement. Quick, convenient foods need a lot of pre-processing before they reach us, which in turn often means using additives and extra sugar and salt.

What your body needs

Proteins break down to create chemicals that act as neurotransmitters.

Simple carbohydrates like sugar give a quick burst of energy, and fats are needed to keep neural networks healthy and so are good for your memory.

Salts are essential for all human cells to function, but need to be the right balance of sodium and potassium.

Fibre, vitamins and trace elements all play essential roles in keeping us healthy.

Grazing

It all adds up to making sure that you eat a range of foods every day. The traditional Western approach of three meals a day is giving way to a 'little and often' approach. 'Grazing' allows the whole body to receive a steadier supply of oxygenated blood and so the brain maintains a more constant state of alertness.

A big meal makes us feel sleepy because our digestive system takes more blood to enable it to function and so our brain doesn't get enough until the meal is digested. As long as you graze mainly on healthier, unprocessed foods, and drink plenty of water, you will maintain energy and performance throughout the day.

SLEEPING

As adults we need an average of eight hours sleep a night. Over time, lack of sleep can lead to poor concentration, low energy and mood swings or even mental ill health. Without enough sleep, our brains do not function at their full capacity.

Quality not quantity

Most people seem to need less sleep as they get older, but many of us impose sleep deprivation on ourselves long before we age by working too late, eating badly late in the day and not exercising. And it is not just the amount of sleep that counts – the quality is important too.

Your brain needs time to process all that has happened during the day, and it does this during periods of deep sleep, or REM (Rapid Eye Movement). The particular neurotransmitter that produced during REM helps keep neural networks healthy and so improves the memory-forming process. So when we say we'll 'sleep on it', we actually do – the brain lays down memory traces while we sleep so that when we wake, it becomes easier to solve the problems we were wrestling with the night before.

Research has shown that a common cause of sleep disruption is a drop in blood sugar levels in the night. A non-sugary snack before you go to bed may help. Bananas contain a natural sedative, so try eating one about an hour before bedtime, and of course, short relaxation and breathing exercises are also helpful in getting us off to sleep in the first place.

Go to bed on a banana

EXERCISE

Applications for gym membership shoot up after Christmas and other periods of high indulgence, and just before the summer. But most of us know that regular exercise throughout the week, and the year, will be better for us than an occasional binge.

What if you haven't time to exercise? Either you have to take time to be healthy or you have to take time to be ill.

There are far too many exercise options to list here. Find something that suits you, and if possible, find someone to do it with. The worry about letting the other person down might act as an added incentive to keep going. Schedule exercise into your diary, just as you do an evening out with friends.

FUN

This can be a word to strike terror into the heart: 'Come on, it'll be fun. Don't be a spoilsport.' Enjoyment is a very personal commodity. Paintballing, tapestry, making model boats, Chinese cooking, learning ancient Greek and country dancing can all be great fun, but only if you enjoy them.

The important thing is to make time for some enjoyment, whatever it is. Research shows that becoming absorbed in something that we enjoy significantly reduces stress levels. In addition, laughter actually leads to a decrease in the amount of cortisol – the stress hormone – that we produce and improves the immune system.

Work to music

Many 'fun' activities engage different parts of the brain to those that we use when working and so help our brain fitness. Listening to music, for example, involves both sides of the brain in processing melodies and rhythms. We may well produce better ideas after a session working on our favourite creative hobby than if we'd sat down thinking hard and seriously about it.

ANSWERS

Pages 8–9 Warm-up

1 30

2 18 (Prime number + 1)

3 Tee, tea; two, too; whole, hole; scene, seen; banned, band; male, mail; vain, vein; tacked, tact

4 3

5 36 (tree = 9, flower = 6, vegetable = 10, fruit = 11)

6 MH

7 Mr Carpenter is a painter,

Mr Mason is a carpenter,

Mr Painter is a mason

8 Room 14 (Consonants = 1, vowels = 3)

9 A _____ **E F** ____ **H I**

      B C D _____ **G** _____ **J**

10 TRIP 1: Cat to car – back empty-handed

TRIP 2: Roger to car – back with cat

TRIP 3: Sara to car – back empty-handed

TRIP 4: Cat to car

Pages 22–23 Limber up

A piece of cake: 3

All in the family: 5

Count on it: 7

Lost letters: H, T, B, R
Country code: 10 (consonants = 2, vowels = 1)
Lucky 13:   TWELVE + ONE
Follow on: 18, 43 (+ 4, + 8, + 4, + 8 etc.)
Odd one out: 4 (August, January, March, Tuesday, July, September)

Page 76 Test your semantic memory

Oslo, Ankara, Nairobi, Montevideo, Lhasa, Canberra, Riyadh, Bucharest, Sofia, Seoul, Damascus, Nicosia, Khartoum, Managua, Quito, Bogotà, Bangkok, Caracas

Page 99 What do you see?

Possible answers: a Mexican on a tightrope, necklace, fried egg on a line, stuffed olive on a skewer, tunnel, alien's eye

Pages 115–116

1 a) Please tell me your answer by Friday.

b) We are still short staffed.

c) We will not be able to do this for quite a while.

d) The suppliers did not give us an adequate reason for the delay.

e) We will have to find new ways to achieve our objectives.

2 a) disinterested b) fewer c) formerly d) affect e) stationery

3 a) Seven out of ten people can operate the new system.

b) I agree with some of Sue's points.

c) Please can you help me work out how much paper we'll need.

d) It's best to wait for George to be in a receptive mood.

e) I have a different idea.

Page 121 Daily workout plan

1 Use liquid to float it out; Suck it out (with or without a vacuum cleaner);
Put a stick down with glue on the end

4 G, S, M (Game, Set and Match)

7 12 (It is not a prime number)

Pages 122–123 Analytical and logical thinking

1 44 (square = 13, circle = 8, triangle = 11, pentagon = 12)

2 STRANGE

3 Wz5, Yx3

4 D

5 Wine glass (not enough rings)

6 H = 1, I = 2, J = 3, K = 4, M = 6, N = 7, P = 9, Q = 0

7 7 ways

8 6 + 7 + 8 + 9 = 30

8 + 7 + 6 + 5 = 26

9 D

Page 127 At least once a week

1 LASAGNE, GOULASH, MOUSSAKA, PAELLA, CURRY, HAMBURGER, OMELETTE, RAVIOLI, ENCHILADAS

2 1 down: XS, 2 down: LA

3 a) aromatic plant b) a duck c) a wood d) a dog e) a cheese
f) an animal that feeds on meat and vegetation g) a semi-precious stone
h) used to pluck strings on a musical instrument i) sweet pepper

4 HEAD HELD HELL TELL TALL TAIL

5 a) partridge/cartridge b) mortal/portal c) pine/mine d) minute/linnet)
e) garden/harden f) grand/spanned

6 a) INK b) ATE c) AND

7 potatoes, hooves, reefs, deer, allies, alleys, journeys, children, oxen,
dances, princesses, audiences

8 bear/bare; made/maid; tied/tide; aid/aide; loan/lone; time/thyme;
ewe/yew; eight/ate; rhyme/rime; find/fined

9 handouts, freight, volley, unsliced, hustling, nectarines, cautioned, pictures,
angrier, epitaphs, reduction, provides

10 box, duck, bear, right, pine, flat, grate, knot

Page 130 Tone up your mathematical intelligence

1 91 (81 from the first 729, then 9 from the 81, then 1 from the 9)

2 40 (3 x 8 + 4 squared)

3 $23.43

4 D

5 45 litres

6 64

7 2400

8 18

9 one-third of 138

INDEX

A

acronyms 81
activist style learning 30
adrenal glands 70
adrenaline 69, 88
ageing, brains 21
alcohol 134
alertness 77
alpha brain waves 98
Alzheimer's disease 70
analytical thinking 25
    exercises 122–3
anti-creativity 104
assertiveness skills 48
attention, paying 84
attitude, positive 104
Augustine of Hippo, St 10
axons 12

B

bananas 136
beta brain waves 98
Binet, Alfred 18
body language 111
brain
    ageing 21
    anatomy 11
    cells 12, 69
    gender differences 20
    hemispheres 13
    senses 14–17
brain waves 98
brainstorming 56
Brayshaw 80–1
breathing 93

C

caffeine 134
cerebral cortex 11
communication
    exercises 115–17
    ideas 108–17
    meetings 114–15
    preparation 112–13
    questionnaire 108–9

speed 132
    types 110–11
competences 34–41
concentration 49–51
convergent thinking 97
cortex 11, 15
cortisol 70, 88, 137
crazy headlines, learning
    techniques 80–1
creative thinking 25
creativity 96–107
    exercises 121
CRISP, objectives 66
cultural barriers 53

D

daily exercises 121–6
dehydration 134
delta brain waves 98
dendrites 12
Descartes, René 14
development plan 120
diet 134, 135
digit span memory test 74
distractions 44, 51
    see also concentration
divergent thinking 97
drinking 134

E

ears 16
eating 135
emotional intelligence 19
    exercises 131
emotions 52–3, 69
enjoyment 137
environmental intelligence 19
    exercises 131
episodic memory 75
exercise 83, 95, 136–7
exercises
    analytical thinking 122–3
    communication 115–17
    creativity 121
    daily 121–6

intelligences 130–1
lateral thinking 121
linguistic intelligence 127–9
logical thinking 122–3
memory 83–5, 125–6
mental dexterity 22–3
senses 124
verbal communication 115–16
visual communication 116–17
vocal communication 116
warm up 8–9, 42–3
weekly 127–31
work-life balance 133
experience
    learning from 29
    previous 26
explanations, alternative
    98–9
explicit memory 69

F

Feeling (F) personality type
    32–3, 60
feelings 52–3, 69
filing 45
five-minute rest cure 94
food 135
frameworks, learning techniques
    78–82
fun 137

G

Gardner, Howard 18, 97
gender differences 20
Goleman, Daniel 18
grazing 135
group-thinking sessions 106–7

H

Hadamard 96
hard-to-get-at memories 82
health 134–7
hearing 16, 124
Honey, Peter 30
hormones 69, 70, 88, 137

I

ideas
  communicating 108–17
  creativity 96–107
implementability, solutions 58–9
implicit memory 69
inspiration 105
intelligence 18–19
  exercises 131
Intelligence Quotient (IQ) 18, 21
interruptions 46–8
iNtuiting (N) personality type
  32–3, 60
IQ (Intelligence Quotient) 18, 21
issues, identifying
  see problem-solving

J

job applications 36–7
journey to work 42
Jung, Carl 32

K

Kline, Nancy 61
knowledge, semantic memory 76

L

language 110, 115–16
lateral thinking, exercises 121
laughter 137
learning 29–31
  diary 118–19
  memory 77, 78
  styles 30
  techniques 78–82
left hemisphere, brain 13
linguistic intelligence 19
  exercises 127–9
logical thinking, exercises 122–3
long-term memory 75–6
Lucas, Bill 18

M

magic wand technique 55
mammalian brain 11
Maslow, A.H. 64
mathematical intelligence 19
  exercises 130
medication 83
meditation 94–5
meetings 62, 114–15
memory 68–85

exercises 83–5, 125–6
  failure of 70
  long-term 75–6
  recall techniques 77–82
  reliability 71
  reviewing 85
  short-term 72–4
  stress 70
  types 69
memory cards 103
metaphors 101–2
motivation 64–5, 67
  memory 77
motor cortex 15
motor nerves 15
movement 15
Mumford, Alan 30
music 137
musical intelligence 19
  exercises 131

N

names, remembering 82
needs 64–5
neurons 12, 69, 70
non-verbal communication 111,
  117
nonsense phrases, learning
  techniques 81
noradrenaline 69
nutrition 135

O

objectives 66–7

P

paralanguage 110–11
Parkinson's disease 70
patterns, learning techniques
  78–82
pegwords, learning techniques 80
perception 15, 52
personal competence,
  questionnaire 38–40
personality types 32–3
phonological loop 73
physical exercise 83, 95, 136–7
physical intelligence 19
  exercises 131
Poincarré 96
positive attitude 104
practical intelligence 19

exercises 131
pragmatist style learning 30
primitive brain 11
problem-solving
  implementability 58–9
  reframing 54–5
  stepping-stone guide 56–7
  whole person model 60–3
procedural memory 76
prospective memory 76

Q

questionnaires
  communications 108–9
  personal competence 38–40
  stress 89–90
  thinking skills 27–8
questions, reverse 103

R

random word connections 100–1
recall techniques 77–82
reflector style learning 30
reframing 54–5
relaxation 93–5
reverse questions 103
reviewing
  learning 118–19
  memory 85
right hemisphere, brain 13

S

self-assessment 118
semantic memory 76
senses 14–17
  exercises 124
Sensing (S) personality type
  32–3, 60
sex differences see gender
  differences
short-term memory 72–4
sight 16, 124
Simonides 78
skin 17
sleep 136
SMART, objectives 66
smell 17, 124
social intelligence 19
  exercises 131
solutions see problem-
  solving
Sperry, Roger 13

spiritual intelligence 19
   exercises 131
stepping-stone guide, problem-
   solving 56–7
Stern, William 18
stress 86–95
   competence 88
   levels 87
   memory 70
   questionnaire 89–90
   signs 86–7
   thinking 88
stress drivers 89–92
synapses 69

T
taste 17, 124
technology 132
telephone 48
ten-second holiday 93
theorist style learning 30
theta brain waves 98
thinking

blocks to 52
creativity 25, 97
   exercises 122–3
   group sessions 106–7
   learning styles 29–31
   personality types 32–3
   questionnaire 27–8
   stress 88
   types 24–33
thinking climate 61–3
Thinking (T) personality type
   32–3, 60
time logs 47
touch 17, 124

V
values, stress drivers 91
verbal communication 110
   exercises 115–16
verbalization, learning techniques
   81
visual communication 111
   exercises 116–17

visual cortex 16
visual intelligence 19
   exercises 131
visual memory trace 73
visualization 82, 94–5
vocabularies 110
vocal communication 110–11
   exercises 116
voicemails 48

W
walk round the house, learning
   technique 78–80
water, drinking 134
weekly exercises 127–31
whole person model, problem-
   solving 60–3
work spaces 44
work-life balance 132–3
   exercises 133

Z
Zohar, Danah 18

FURTHER INFORMATION

The Thinking Environment
Time to Think Inc.
UK: 63, Preston Crowmarsh,
Wallingford, Oxfordshire,
OX10 6SL
US: 6004, Rhode Island Avenue,
Riverdale, MD 20737
www.timetothink.com

The Myers-Briggs
Personality Type Indicator
UK: Oxford Psychologists Press
Ltd, Elsfield Hall, 15–17 Elsfield
Way, Oxford OX2 8EP,
www.opp.co.uk
US: Consulting Psychologists
Press Inc., 3808, East Bayshore
Road, Pao Alto, CA 94303,
ww.cpp-db.com

Learning Styles
UK: Peter Honey Learning, 10,
Linden Avenue, Maidenhead,
Berkshire, SL6 6HB,
www.peterhoneylearning.com

RESOURCES

Kay Barwick, Liferoots:
The Hilltop Model,
see page 113.

Frames of Mind: The Theory
of Multiple Intelligences
Howard Gardner, Basic Books,
New York, 1983

Emotional Intelligence: Why
it Can Matter More Than IQ
Daniel Goleman, Bloomsbury,
London, 1996

Taibi Kahler. Recipient of the
1977 Eric Berne Memorial
Scientific Award for his work on
miniscript and the five drivers.

Time to Think: Listening
to Ignite the Human Mind
Nancy Kline, Ward Lock,
London, 1999

Power up your Mind
Bill Lucas, Nicholas Brealey,
London, 2001

Motivation and Personality
Abraham Maslow, Harper and
Row, New York, 1970

SQ: Spiritual Intelligence,
the Ultimate Intelligence
Danah Zohar and Ian Marshall,
Bloomsbury, London, 2000

ACKNOWLEDGEMENTS

original edition
Executive Editor: **Trevor Davies**
Editor: **Rachel Lawrence**
Design Manager: **Tokiko Morishima**
Design: **Martin Topping at 'ome**
Illustrations: **David Beswick at 'ome**
Production Controller: **Jo Sim**

pyramid edition
Executive Editor: **Trevor Davies**
Editor: **Kate Tuckett**
Executive Art Editor: **Karen Sawyer**
Designer: **'ome Design**
Production Controller: **Nosheen Shan**